THE FINANCE DOCTOR

"We have always been intimidated by this subject, but Dr. Dink really made things easy to understand. And because the steps were part of an interesting story, we found ourselves turning the pages quickly, anxious to learn more and more."

—Hans Rehme, police officer, and
Caryn Rehme, teacher,
Ophelia, VA

"The anecdotes used in the book make the diagnosis much more personal and meaningful than the cold impersonal opinions doled out by so many financial 'experts.' Dr. Dink's stories are not only entertaining, but also make finance very easy to understand."

—Gaylyne Hadlock, telcom specialist,
Dallas, TX

"San Francisco has a great quality of life, but it also has a high cost of living. Dr. Dink's suggestions have made it possible for my money to grow, which means I don't have to choose between making a living and having a life."

—Steve Mitzenmacher, business development,
San Francisco, CA

"Dr. Dink is the 'Kerouac of Finance.' He doesn't confuse his readers with financial jargon and supplies them with examples relative to their own experiences."

—Keisha Carter, student,
Aliquippa, PA

"As a physician-in-training, I have incurred so much educational debt that I used to feel like I'd never get out of the hole. Dr. Dink's formula, Q-Q-Kachoo, taught me how to make sound decisions that have led to peace of mind about my future."

—Adam Vella, M.D.,
Brooklyn, NY

"Before reading *The Finance Doctor,* I was contemplating whether to buy or lease a new car. Not only did Dr. Dink help me with my buy/lease decision, but he also gave me the advice I needed to pay off all my credit card debt and make investments for the future. Thanks to Dr. Dink, I am debt free and have a financially stable future."

—Leslie Cline, banking analyst,
Charlotte, NC

"The book has a lot of humor, which makes it easy to read. It's good for people of all ages because it's never too late to start investing or too early to learn good habits."

—Michelle and Herb Woland, retired,
Sarasota, FL

"The first person I recommended *The Finance Doctor* to was my sister, after she asked me to help her fill out her 401(k) form. Now that I am at the Harvard Business School, everyone asks me for advice about their finances. My answer is simple: Ask Dr. Dink!"

—Marc Bruno, student,
Boston, MA

THE FINANCE DOCTOR

An 8-Step Prescription
So You Can
Stop Chasing Your Bills &
Start Chasing Your Dreams

DR. DINK
with Frank R. Scatoni

Vital Publishing
Palm Beach, FL

ISBN 0-9703811-0-7

The authors have performed extensive research, yet they assume no responsibility for errors, inaccuracies, or any inconsistency herein. Any slights of people or organizations are unintentional. Investments are inherently risky, and the authors make no guarantee as to individual results. Readers should consult financial experts for specific advice about their individual circumstances.

Printed in the United States of America.

For volume discounts, contact:
Vital Publishing
3400 S. Ocean Blvd. Suite 3B-2
Palm Beach, FL 33480

Cover design by Smay Vision
Photo of Dr. Dink by Blanken Photography
Edited by Peter T. Fornatale
Text design by Tina Thompson

Visit us online at http://www.doctordink.com
Logo and www.doctordink.com designed by carterdesignworks

I have moved around a lot in my life, and at each stop, I've always had a roommate. Aside from the friendships and bonds that have formed, having a roommate has been the best financial decision I have ever made. And so . . .

This book is dedicated to all my roommates

(In order of appearance)

ROOMMATE	PLACE	BIRTHPLACE
Erlaine Klaff Bernstein, my mom, for her unconditional love.	Potomac, MD	Baltimore, MD
Art Dinkin, my dad, for never steering me wrong.	Potomac, MD	Washington, D.C.
Andy Dinkin, my big brother, who always held me to a higher standard.	Potomac, MD	Silver Spring, MD
Bryan Blanken, for convincing me that people want choices, not orders.	Kauffman Camp	Washington, D.C.
Chris Martin, for encouraging me to take my foot off the brakes.	Ithaca, NY	Highland Falls, NY
Andy Hite, for showing me how to make my own luck.	Ithaca, NY	Yonkers, NY
Mike Sandler, for teaching me how to show, instead of tell.	Ithaca, NY	Valley Stream, NY
Greg Knopp, for free legal advice and pure comedy.	Ithaca, NY	New Rochelle, NY
Greg Greene, for still not *getting it.*	Ithaca, NY	White Plains, NY

Jeff Woodring, who reminded me that "I was not put on this earth to make a living."

Ithaca, NY Rochester, NY

Shawn Cole, for teaching me the power of forgiveness.

Ithaca, NY Hudson, WI

Bryan Blanken, for finally buying me those Cokes I won from him at Kauffman Camp.

Las Vegas, NV Washington, D.C.

Shawn Fox, who showed me the rewards of working for myself.

Ithaca, NY Blytheville, AR

Tim Barry, for believing in me every step of the way.

Ithaca, NY Manitowoc, WI

Kathryn Dinkin, my stepmom, for all the reality checks.

Rockville, MD Plymouth, NC

Jason Lorber, for encouraging me to get out of "the trap" and move out West.

Bethesda, MD Los Angeles, CA

Jason Freeland, my cousin, for showing me that it's possible to beat the odds.

Beverly Hills, CA Baltimore, MD

Greg Lanesey, for showing me the life of a writer.

Los Angeles, CA Waterbury, CT

Marty Walsh, for showing me how much fun it is to play the guitar.

Destrehan, LA State College, PA

Marc Bruno, for helping me shape the content of the book and the lyrics to my song.

Atlanta, GA Park Ridge, IL

Lance Sprinkle, for giving me the nicest compliment in the world.

Atlanta, GA Albany, NY

Todd Solan, who still writes me three-page e-mails every time I ask for feedback.

Tempe, AZ Paterson, NJ

Jimbo Patterson, for showing me that "these are the days."

San Diego, CA Blytheville, AR

Charlie Beard, for helping me turn an idea into a career.

San Diego, CA Bellingham, WA

Alex Panelli, for teaching me to embrace technology.

Tempe, AZ Santa Clara, CA

Tim Barry, who finally admitted that, in college, it wasn't water that he spilled in my bed.

Chicago, IL Manitowoc, WI

Marvin Bernstein, my stepdad, for teaching me how to value a stock and how to catch a football.

Osprey, FL Washington, D.C.

Mike "Stucky" Stuckert and *Bill "Worm" Vincent,* for introducing me to Ronnie Woo-Woo.

Wrigleyville, IL Highland, IN ("The Reeg")

Mike Kelly, for teaching me the path of the Peaceful Warrior.

New York, NY New York, NY

Dr. Darren Carpizo, who encourages me to follow my passion, work hard, and play hard.

Santa Monica, CA Evanston, IL

And most of all . . .

To my Grandpa Harry and late Grandma Tillie, for their sense of humor and love of life.

Contents

THE FINANCE DOCTOR

Introduction

The Trap

If you can do anything setting out, or along the way—because it's never too late to start again—figure out who you are. What do you love to do? How do you want to live? Then, don't let a career drive you, let passion drive your life.

—Randy Komisar

Just about everything I know about financial therapy I learned from my parents. I know that might seem strange, especially since neither my mom nor my dad ever went to business school or held a job on Wall Street, but it's true. My folks didn't teach me about IRAs, 401(k)s, mutual funds, money market accounts, stocks, bonds, and all that other financial mumbo jumbo. Anyone could have taught me that stuff, and as it turned out, learning the financial mumbo jumbo was the easy part. What my parents did teach me, however, were three simple steps that have become the very foundation of my financial therapy. I call those three steps *Q-Q-Kachoo.*

Now before you start scratching your head and conjuring up images of John, Paul, George, and Ringo, let me be the first to tell you that my Q-Q-Kachoo has absolutely nothing to do with the Beatles song "I Am the Walrus." It has to do with making decisions. Fortunately for me, I had the advantage of learning from perhaps the greatest decision maker that ever roamed the earth. It is no small coincidence that this legendary individual just happens to be my mom.

Here's how it all started.

My brother, Andy, didn't start playing tackle football until the tenth grade. He was always a decent athlete and an okay student, but he was one of those kids who were destined to go to a local college. After struggling as a sophomore on the junior varsity team, he devoted just about every second of every day lifting weights and running. In spite of his tenacious work ethic, he still shocked everyone when he was selected All-State after his junior year. Before you knew it, big-time schools were fawning over the kid who had been playing football for only two years. Andy thrived on all the attention, and made up his mind that he was going to get a football scholarship, or at least die trying. And when Andy made up his mind to do something, very little could get in his way. A consummate competitor and budding salesman, Andy had a plan.

After the last school day of his junior year of high school, Andy laid out on the kitchen table each and every recruiting letter that he had received from colleges. There were more than three hundred letters from high-profile schools such as Alabama, Penn State, Stanford, Michigan, UCLA, Duke, North Carolina, Texas, and Maryland. As a naive ninth grader, I wasn't sure what was about to happen, but Andy told me something big was in the works. A seasoned negotiator, my mom didn't take Andy's "recruitment-letter" bait and she simply chose to wait for him to make the first move.

Drawing on his skills as an All-State defensive tackle, my brother decided that a quick attack might catch the opponent—in this case, my mom—off guard. He waited for her to check on the macaroni so he could make his pitch without having to make eye contact. Nonchalantly, he said, "Mom, Coach Shepherd told me today that the only thing that could prevent me from getting a scholarship is an injury."

But my brother forgot whom he was dealing with. My mom is a heck of a lot smarter than the average bear, and unlike my brother, she's never one to beat around the bush. "All right, buster boy, what do you want?" she said, seemingly reading my brother's mind.

To this day, I still marvel at my mom's instincts. I suppose if you spent five years dealing with divorce attorneys, as she did, you too would be able to smell a rat. My mom knew my brother had something up his sleeve, and she wasn't about to play along. "Out with it already," she said, as I sat at the table waiting for my macaroni and cheese, doing everything I could to keep quiet.

Fighting his own nervousness, Andy tried to convince my mom that he needed to devote every minute of his summer to working out. So instead of getting a summer job—which is something my brother and I always had to do—he argued that training for football was a job in and of itself and there was just no way he could get a scholarship unless he committed his whole summer to training. He stressed Coach Shepherd's words and cited some statistic about injuries being the result of a lack of preparation.

Normally, I would have never kept my mouth shut, but I had promised my brother I wouldn't butt in. Even so, my mind couldn't help wandering. As much as I was rooting for my brother, I didn't think he had a prayer in the world. As a single parent, my mother needed all the help she could get and was never shy about asking us to pitch in. I was convinced that she would just tell Andy that if she had enough hours in the day to work full-time and still raise us crazy kids, then he could certainly find enough time to work out before or after his day job as a camp counselor.

To my surprise, she didn't tell him that at all. In fact, she didn't tell him anything. Instead, she went over to the stove and pretended to stir the macaroni. At the time, I couldn't imagine what she was doing, but looking back on it, it all makes perfect sense. She was merely stalling—stalling so she could do what she did best: make a decision.

Even for those who know my mom well, it is easy to overlook

this skill. The woman is not only loud, but very emotional, and to an outside observer, she might sometimes seem on the brink of insanity. But for those who really know her, and I put myself at the top of that list, the woman epitomizes the 3 Cs—calm, cool, and collected. Sure, she is bright, but I've learned in life that being bright is overrated. Think about it: How many straight-A students do you know who don't have a lick of common sense? What I find to be underrated in life is the ability to harness knowledge into sound decision making. As far as this goes, no one can touch my mom.

While she thought, Andy continued to stare at the letters. I could sense his imagination running wild. He gazed down, and my eyes followed his: *Alabama, Penn State, Stanford, Michigan, UCLA, Duke, North Carolina, Texas,* and *Maryland.* All the while, my mom continued to "stir" the macaroni. Looking back, I'm sure this was something she did for every big decision in her life, but it was the first time I ever really witnessed the process. It has stuck with me ever since.

Years later, I asked her what she had been thinking about. When she said, "Q-Q-Kachoo," I remember saying, "Gesundheit." After a deep breath and a warm smile, my mom said, "Thank you, but I didn't sneeze. I said 'Q-Q-Kachoo.'" Then she went on to explain the magical formula.

My mom has a funny way of explaining things, so I'll do my best to translate. She has a way of talking in songs and clichés, which can be downright hilarious—but to someone outside the family, rather difficult to decipher. She started her explanation by citing my grandmother: "Remember what Grandma Tillie used to say: 'Rich or poor, it's good to have money.' That's why you've got to look at the numbers first. The first *Q* stands for Quantitative. It's just a fancy way of saying, *'Do the numbers first, stupid.'*"

It made perfect sense to me to start with the numbers. Many of our biggest life decisions involve money in one way or another.

Whether it's buying a house or buying a car, paying for a child's tuition, or taking the dream vacation of our lives, each and every one of our decisions will impact our pocketbook whether we want it to or not. In my brother's case, the numbers were very simple. By working as a camp counselor, he would have made $2,000. While that would have been a decent chunk of change to put into the family's household budget, it wasn't $2,000 that we absolutely could not live without. On the other hand, a full scholarship to a decent university at that time was worth about $80,000. My mom didn't have to be a poker player to know that the payoff would be 40 to 1.

The next thing my mother did was *consult Ben Franklin.* No, Ben Franklin isn't the name of my great-uncle who lives in Philadelphia, and he's not the neighbor next door who is obsessed with flying kites. I'm talking about the real Ben Franklin, one of our nation's founding fathers. My mom isn't much for history, but she had picked up a great technique during one of her many sales jobs. She explained, "People don't feel good about buying something unless they have all the facts. Plus, it makes them more comfortable about buying when you come across as objective." I understood what she meant, but couldn't help but ask, "Mom, what does that have to do with the second Q—or Ben Franklin, for that matter?"

"The second *Q* stands for Qualitative," she said. "It's just a fancy word for the other factors that are not related to numbers. You see, whenever good old Ben had to make an important decision, he would simply take out a piece of parchment and draw a straight line down the middle. On one side he would write the pros, and on the other side he would write the cons. He then listed all the factors that went into making his decision."

Looking back, it's pretty obvious that while my mom was pretending to stir the macaroni, she was actually doing a Q-Q-Kachoo in her head. In this instance, her mental list probably shaped up like this:

Pros of Summer Football Training	**Cons of Summer Football Training**
Training increases the chance of a scholarship.	Our family could use the $2,000 he would make as a camp counselor.
Training reduces the chance of injury during the season.	Our family needs that $2,000 he would make as a camp counselor.
If I let him do what he wants, he'll enjoy his summer and have no regrets.	Our family *really* needs that $2,000 he would make as a camp counselor.

After doing the numbers and consulting Ben Franklin, my mom was two-thirds closer to making her big decision. I remember thinking at the time that my mom was probably focused on the money. If I were in her shoes, my first thoughts probably would have been on paying the bills. But as I said, my mom was calm, cool, and collected and had the presence of mind to see the big picture.

The pros side had more to do with my brother's dreams and with his being happy. The cons side had to do with money and nothing else. Had it not been for the second Q—consulting Ben Franklin—she would have made her decision based solely on money. True to her own words, she knew that she had to have all the facts. But my mom also has been known to say, "Facts schmacts. Sometimes you've got to throw out all that rational junk and just trust your instincts." And this is why the last step of my mom's three-step process is so important—*she did a gut check.*

Don't ask me how she came up with the word "Kachoo," but don't read into it too much. It's just her funny way of saying, "Check your gut." In this case, she looked inside her heart before coming to a conclusion. There was just no way that $2,000 was going to prevent her firstborn from chasing his dreams. As she always used to say—and believe me, my mom always meant what she said—"I'd go through fire and water for my children." Compared to fire and water, I suppose two grand was just a drop in the bucket.

I can't emphasize enough how much thought my mom would put into decisions. She knew that no matter how many times Andy could bench-press three hundred pounds, there was still no way to guarantee that he would get a full scholarship. Plus, she didn't want to give my brother the impression that sports came before education. So although she agreed to let him off the hook as a camp counselor, she saddled him with another task: He would have to study.

This decision really brought home three characteristics that best define my mom. First and foremost, she always believed in my brother and me and encouraged us to chase our dreams. Second, she always stressed education. I can still hear her saying over and over, "There is no trust fund. There is no family business to run. The only thing you can depend on is your education. If you want to go to college, I'll scrub floors if I have to, but I'm not going to spend a cent to send you to the thirteenth grade." I never quite knew what she meant by the thirteenth grade, but by the way she said it, I didn't exactly want to find out.

The last characteristic, and the one that we always marvel at, is that my mom never paid full price for anything. So, as part of the agreement to let my brother train for football, she insisted that he take an SAT prep course offered by the county for $50. Football scholarship or no football scholarship, my mom was going to make darn sure that Andy scored well enough on the college entrance exam to at least get accepted to a decent school. She was sharp enough to know that most colleges care about a lot more than just blocking and tackling.

The fact that my mom made my brother take an affordable SAT prep class—one that was available to every student—is just another example of her prudent thinking. While other kids paid thousands of dollars for private tutors, my mom impressed upon Andy that it wasn't how much she spent that would get him a good test score, but how hard he worked to accomplish the goal.

Andy devoted his entire summer to working out and studying, and he received the fruits of his labor. By Thanksgiving of that year, he had received scholarship offers from all of the major powerhouses. Looking back, I can tell you that my mom's decision may have been the most monumental in family history. Had she been impulsive and not gone through that process she named Q-Q-Kachoo, who knows what would become of Andy. But I have to think that getting a full scholarship to UNC–Chapel Hill, being selected All–Atlantic Coast Conference for both football and academics, making lifelong friends, and laying the foundation for a successful career in business would have been pretty tough to beat.

It makes me sad that I now realize that my brother is in the minority. Very few of us, whether it be kids, students, parents, or grandparents, are presented with the opportunity to chase our dreams. Paying the bills is a reality most of us can't escape from. As my mom always used to ask, "You think there's a money tree growing in our backyard?"

I sadly learned that, indeed, money does not grow on trees and that it often stands in the way of our dreams. I hear the word *reality* a lot. I don't dismiss it, but I can't help but urge my students to look at the big picture. I don't tell them what decision to make, but I do remind them that decision making is a three-step process and money is only one factor. After all, had my mom only been thinking about money, Andy's two favorite words would probably have been "What if?"

From this experience as well as many others, I have come up with a prescription for financial therapy. The road was a long and bumpy one, but well worth the trip. In fact, my story is worth telling because everything I did—and didn't do, for that matter—helped shape the formula that I prescribe today.

Who Is Dr. Dink and How Did He Fall into "the Trap"?

Upon meeting someone for the first time, we have a tendency to size that person up and put him or her into a "box." When people start peppering me with questions about my background, job history, and the places I lived, I sometimes want to say, "How about I fax you a résumé and you figure it out for yourself?" It's not that these questions are unfair, it's just that I know the person is trying to form a picture of who I am based on limited information. If that's the case, I know they are going to end up confused.

Am I a rich kid from Potomac, Maryland, who went to high school with the sons of Sugar Ray Leonard, Jack Kemp, and other Washington, D.C., elite? The kid whose parents got him just about everything he wanted—Nike sneakers, Polo shirts, basketball camp, summer camp, and exchange programs to France and Costa Rica? The kid whose parents paid to send him to the Ivy League and who received a six-month internship where he lived in five-star hotels all over the world? The kid with the MBA who went on to make six figures for a prestigious consulting firm and saved enough money to quit his job and move to a penthouse on Madison Avenue in Manhattan to chase his dreams of becoming a teacher and a writer?

Or am I the kid whose parents got divorced when he was eight and heard the word "no" so much that he stopped asking for material things? The kid who started working for a dollar a day when he was eight, making beds and tying shoes at a neighbor's nursery and taking every job under the sun? The kid who got a work permit the day he turned fourteen and started washing dishes for $3.35 an hour and umpiring softball games and shoveling driveways to have some pocket money? The kid who applied for dozens of scholarships, worked as a cook, and took summer school to graduate from Cornell early and save a year's tuition? The kid who "hustled" money by selling windows and playing in underground poker games to earn some extra cash? The kid who put himself through a public MBA program and put his best friend through two years of design school?

The answer is yes to all of the above. Stockbrokers classify high-net-worth individuals as those with more than $100,000 in liquid assets. I have never come close to that, but I have never been one to worry about how others classify me. In my own eyes, I am financially healthy. Which brings me to my definition of good financial health—being in the position to chase your dreams and not your bills.

After I graduated from business school, I had $25,000 worth of credit card debt as a result of poor decision making. I hated my job as a management consultant, but reality dictated that I punch the clock and pay the bills. I knew what it was like to feel stuck, but I refused to accept it. I also knew that sound financial health was the first step in allowing me to chase my dreams.

To make some sense of all this, once again look no further than my parents. After my folks split up when I was eight, my mom's net income, including child support, was around $25,000. She still managed to pay the mortgage and the property taxes on a house in Montgomery County, Maryland, one of the wealthiest counties in the United States. My brother and I never did without. My mom would have it no other way, even at her own expense.

One occasion that comes to mind happened during my junior year of high school. After putting a ten-dollar bill a week in an old coffee jar for two years, my mom had saved $1,000 and was all set to take a vacation and spend a week in Acapulco. A week before her trip, she found out that my high school was offering an exchange program to Costa Rica. Without thinking twice, she canceled her trip and sent in the deposit for mine. The reason she didn't have to think twice was that she had a vision. Remember—all she ever wanted was to see her kids get the best education possible. She was not about to let an umbrella in a strawberry daiquiri override her desire to see me further my education.

In terms of decision making, my dad's no slouch either. He doesn't own a shirt marked "dry-clean only" and he has never purchased a new car. When he got divorced in 1980, he had to rent his own apartment, pay thousands of dollars in legal fees, and pay child support. And he still found room in his budget to contribute to our college funds and take us to the beach every summer.

To this day, neither of my parents has ever bought something that they couldn't afford. Neither has ever carried a balance on their credit card. They live at outlet malls, discount stores, and half-price nights at restaurants. They use credit cards, but only for convenience, and actually make money on them. My dad gets frequent-flyer miles for his purchases, and my mom gets credit to TJ Maxx and Marshall's so she can save even more on discounted merchandise. Her purse has more coupons than the Sunday paper.

By making good decisions, my parents were never prisoners to money. They had control over their finances, which led to peace of mind. They showed me that when you don't have the burden of debt weighing on your shoulders and you're not so concerned with acquiring material things, you can enjoy and appreciate what you have.

My friend Jimmy often reminds me that the Bible is misquoted. Over lunch one day, he said to me, "The Bible doesn't say that money is the root of all evil. It says that *the love* of money is the root of all evil." My experiences have shown me that money is no more than a piece of paper—an IOU, if you will. Yet I see how it drives people. I used to look out of my apartment on Madison Avenue and see lights in offices twenty-four hours a day. I see a world where the cost to sustain ourselves with food, clothing, and shelter keeps going down, yet we spend more and more time doing the things that we "have to do" so we can consume things that don't bring us any closer to happiness.

My goal is to help you remove money from life's decisions as much as you possibly can. What I am striving for, and what I urge my students to strive for, is Dr. Dink Utopia—D-D-U for short. D-D-U is getting to a place in life where all decisions are made as if money were not an issue. I know it sounds unrealistic, but I have never been much for realism. We live in a society in which we are constantly being told to hedge our bets, to avoid taking risks, and to choose a career that will allow us to make a living. Yuck!

Seeking a Career—Selling Out

In August of 1989, my dad and future stepmom put the top down on Dad's Chrysler LeBaron convertible—bought used, of course—and headed to Ithaca, New York, for freshman orientation at Cornell University. Because the Ivy League doesn't give athletic scholarships, my parents paid $100 to a financial aid specialist who helped me obtain some academic scholarships. But even with that additional money, my parents probably couldn't have afforded to send me there had my brother not received his full scholarship to UNC. Boy, am I glad my mom did that Q-Q-Kachoo.

As a student at Cornell, I worked as a room service waiter at a hotel on campus, took odd jobs during my winter breaks, and took extra credits during summer school at the University of Nevada at Las Vegas so I could graduate early and save almost a year's worth of tuition. Most important, college fulfilled its promise of providing me with the one thing that most of us crave the most—a chance. What it didn't give me was direction.

Upon graduation in 1993, I focused my energy on fulfilling my dream of becoming a teacher and applied to a program called Teach for America (TFA). Modeled after the Peace Corps, TFA gives non–education majors a crash course in how to teach over the summer and then sends them to under-resourced schools in poor communities. Saying I lacked "creativity," the organization rejected me. When I called my dad in tears, his reaction was "You got *rejected*! I thought the only criteria were that you had to be a hundred and seventy-five pounds and dumb enough to want to work for twenty grand in a bad neighborhood." With teaching no longer an option—and little sympathy from my dad—it was time to get a job.

Since my biggest asset was my big mouth, I did the logical thing and became a salesman. I put my heart into selling office products and was often praised by my boss. But after nine months on the job, the only thing I had to show for it was a totaled 1985 Chevy Spectrum. And it wasn't as if I was overspending. I paid my dad a measly $100 a month to live in his basement, drove my mom's old car, and limited my excesses to a Chinese buffet every now and again. Broke and carless, I relied on the "American Way" and used credit to buy a '93 Toyota Camry for $14,000. I put the $700 tax on my credit card, and drove off the lot with sixty payment vouchers for $293 a month. My dad, of course, had tried to talk me out of it, but he took some solace in the fact that I shopped around and bought a "slightly" used car.

Then, in another display of financial bravado, I decided to get my own apartment. If I wasn't saving anything living in my dad's basement *without* a car payment, I certainly wasn't going to be able to afford a $293 car payment and a $400 rent check now that I had moved into an apartment with my buddy Skippy. Looking back, it seems that the only part of the three-step process that I followed was the Kachoo, because I certainly didn't look at the numbers or consult Ben Franklin. But I was young and impressionable, and at least I had a bachelor pad to call my own and a Toyota Camry with gold pinstripes to boot. Little did I know that I had actually fallen into "the trap." Suddenly, at twenty-two, I found myself "selling out."

Now I don't mean "selling out" in the traditional sense of the word—where a person compromises his beliefs, ideals, or artistry for monetary gains—but my definition is pretty similar. In my view, people "sell out" when they get so overwhelmed by their bills that they give up on their dreams to make ends meet. It becomes a vicious cycle where a person compromises his or her passions in life because he or she is so worried about paying the bills.

Most of us have all worried at one time or another about our personal finance. Who has enough money not to worry? Some of us worry about money each and every day of our lives and we can't help but let it cloud our true ambition. We often don't think we are spending too much, but one day we wake up and realize that we have gotten ourselves into a deep hole from which we just can't dig out.

The second I bought that Camry and moved out of my dad's basement, I began to fall into "the trap." I started chasing those car payments and forgot about my dream of becoming a teacher. So many of us spend our whole lives chasing our bills and never getting anywhere—never fulfilling our life's goals because the gas bill is due or our credit card is maxed out. It's not what we dreamed of, but as the saying goes, "We have mouths to feed"—namely, our own!

With the bills mounting, you can only imagine how I jumped at the chance for a new job when my brother recommended that I interview with his friend Glenn—a twenty-five-year-old home-improvement salesman who tooled around town in a cherry-red Porsche. I agreed to go on an appointment with him and listen to his shtick. We zipped around the Beltway as if we were on the Autobahn, while Glenn explained the sales protocol. Just before we entered a potential buyer's one-story home in Greenbelt, Maryland, Glenn cautioned, "Don't say a word—just sit there and smile and watch me make two grand in less than two hours." His used-car-salesman's charm didn't appeal to me, but the fact that he backed up his talk and walked out of the house with a cool $2,300 profit did.

I don't know what shocked me more—that this couple had just spent $8,500 on windows for a tiny house or that they had financed it for over fifteen years. *They never even asked the total price!* All they needed to hear was that the monthly payment was $137. I was probably most surprised by their willingness to buy on the spot without getting other bids, checking up on our company, or at least sleeping on it. Glenn read my naive mind. "People don't buy the total price," he told me, "they buy the monthly payment, and they buy on emotion. If you get people excited enough, they will become impulse buyers. If you can create that emotion, we are going to make a lot of money together."

If making $2,300 in two hours wasn't enough to win me over, I was completely sold after I thumbed through my book of car payments and saw that the last one wasn't due until April 1999. The thought of paying off something for five years didn't sit real well with me. When I told my dad about my new job, he was his usual cynical—although some people would say pragmatic—self. "Son, nobody is going to buy anything from you. It's an unknown company, and you don't know one thing about home improvements." From my dad's perspective, he was giving me good advice. After all, *he* would never buy anything from an unknown company and he would always get at least three bids on any purchase over a thousand dollars.

Thank heavens for me he was wrong! After four months on the job, I learned that not everyone was as wise or as shrewd as my father was when it came to making big purchases. Determined never to be in debt again, I not only paid off the entire balance on my credit card but also paid off the *entire $14,000 balance* on the Camry as well! I only worked about fifteen hours a week, and even then I wasn't really working. I would walk into a stranger's house, ask for a glass of water, shoot the breeze for a couple of hours, and, more often than not, walk out with a check for more than $5,000. If you've ever seen the Barry Levinson movie *Tin Men* with Richard Dreyfuss and Danny DeVito, or even if you haven't, you probably know that home improvement companies have a reputation for going into poor neighborhoods and ripping people off.

What they don't tell you in the movie is that most of the companies, including Glenn's, do great work and give people value for their money. Many of my do-gooder friends said I exploited people, but what they don't realize is that most consumers don't want to be educated buyers. They just want it *right now,* and if the salesman can make the monthly payment affordable, most sign on the dotted line without as much as an arm-twisting.

It's not uncommon to finance $5,000 worth of windows over thirty years so that the monthly payment will only be $84 a month. Do you know that at 20 percent interest, $5,000 worth of windows financed over thirty years ends up costing $30,000? That's right—the interest expense on $5,000 worth of windows is five times the cost of the windows themselves. *That's $25,000 in interest alone!* Is it any wonder the poor stay poor? As Glenn pointed out, most customers don't even look at the final price. The thought of it makes me sick.

It's not the fact that *I did this* to these people that bothers me, it's that I was simply a facilitator for poor decision making. These people were willing to trust a complete stranger with their life savings, or more likely, with money they didn't even have. I'm glad to have had the experience and to have learned from it. What it taught me was that it's not the "system" that needs to be changed or that our country needs more consumer-protection laws. No law in the world can change human nature, and it's human nature to want instant gratification. Even the best education in the world cannot change that, but a quick dose of Q-Q-Kachoo can certainly make us better decision makers.

When I was growing up, my family and I bought most of our clothes at a discount store called Syms. Its motto is "An Educated Consumer Is Our Best Customer." Why everyone doesn't shop there used to be beyond me until I started my research. I learned that most consumers are not educated and don't even seem to care about getting the best price. They buy based on *the here and now.* Whether my do-gooder friends wish to believe this or not, I can tell you from experience that most salesmen do not prey on ignorance and poverty. It's just so easy to prey on impatience, emotion, and greed—all key elements in what I loosely define as human nature.

When it came to windows and siding, it wasn't only the poor neighborhoods where I was selling. As a complete stranger, I would go into the homes of wealthy, college-educated couples, sometimes lawyers and doctors, and walk out with checks for more than $10,000. "Don't these people think to shop around?" my exasperated dad would ask in amazement after I'd rack up another $1,000 commission.

One time I developed such a good rapport with a guy that we had a chew of tobacco together as he told me jokes about West Virginia for an hour. When he agreed to have his siding done for $6,800, he walked into his bedroom and left me in the living room for what seemed like an hour. I figured he was calling a friend, but soon enough, the man whom I had just met that night, and who had never heard of my company, handed me sixty-eight one-hundred-dollar bills. That's right, $6,800 cash! When I counted the money, Benjamin Franklin's stoic grin looked more like a frown.

With tons of time on my hands and plenty of money (no, I didn't keep the cash from this deal), I started playing poker again—a skill that I had picked up during a college internship at the Mirage in Las Vegas. I was doing so well that I considered giving up my sales job to play poker exclusively, until my buddy Wally gave me some of the best advice I've ever heard. "The best way to kill a hot streak," Wally said, "is to give up your day job." I heeded Wally's advice and kept selling—and playing poker on the side. With all the money I was making, all of a sudden job fulfillment didn't seem so important to me.

With my ego getting the best of me, I decided to copy Glenn and buy a Porsche. When I went to grab a catalogue that I had stowed away in my closet, I stumbled across a list of quotes I had been collecting since I was a kid, and read one from the book *Wheels* by Arthur Haley: "You know what that tombstone of yours might say: He did something new, different, worthwhile. He was a leader when they carved new pathways, broke fresh ground. That which he left behind was important and enduring."

Just like that—in one fell swoop my dreams of tooling around town in a cherry red Porsche were dashed. Over the next few days, I constantly asked myself if inhaling a carton of secondhand smoke while trying to decide whether Amarillo Slim was bluffing or not was *important.* When I tried to make myself feel better by saying that improvements to one's home are *enduring,* I thought about that couple in Greenbelt, who with an extra $137 a month payment would soon be *enduring* financial ruin.

I didn't have to think too hard about a profession that I found *worthwhile.* I had just finished tutoring my friend Francis for the SATs, and after six weeks, he improved his score by 240 points. As a result, he was accepted to the college of his choice, and I felt I had actually accomplished something. I thought back to a time in high school when I had tutored my friend Barry for just four hours. His SAT score increased 210 points and he was admitted to the college of his choice as well.

Sadly, neither Barry nor Francis ever graduated from college. Teaching somebody tricks is a quick fix. I taught them how to perform well on a specific test, but I didn't teach them anything they could use in other facets of their life. To this day, those incidents have helped shape my concept of financial therapy—*there are no quick fixes here.* Everything I teach will be applicable to every facet of your life. And if you make the commitment over the long haul, you will experience a dramatic change in your financial well-being.

In four hours, I could give anyone a few pointers on how to get their finances in order. In six weeks, I can do a thorough job of explaining the fundamentals of financial planning. It's unlikely, however, that either would do much good, since real learning is a life-long process. According to behavioral psychologists, it takes forty-five days to break an old habit and start a new one. If I had it to do all over again, I would have given Barry and Francis the tools to become better students. I would have taught them how to study, instead of just giving them the answers.

But even after reading the quote from *Wheels,* the thought of buying a Porsche still hadn't escaped me. Fortunately, a moment of clarity passed over me and I told myself that if I wanted to pursue my passion of teaching, a car payment book with sixty $1,000 vouchers might be tough to afford on twenty grand a year. I decided that doing something I love every day was more important than any amount of horsepower. By not buying the Porsche, I avoided falling into the dreaded trap. Little did I know that just a few years later, I would be back in "the trap" all over again.

Seeking Passion

I once again decided to apply to Teach for America. Determined not to become, as my friend Timmy liked to say, "a two-time loser," I prepared relentlessly for the interview and was accepted. Even though TFA places teachers where they are most needed, I was given a preference and prayed that I would be placed somewhere out west. It was February of 1995, and I had spent ten months selling windows and playing poker and was ready to get out of Washington, D.C. When I told my friend Donald that I was giving up my profitable life as a hustler to become a teacher, he thought I was nuts. "How do you walk away from all that money? You got the life," he said. With no debt, plenty of savings, and no job fulfillment, it was an easy choice to chase my dreams instead of my bills.

I drove from D.C. to Los Angeles to spend a few months out west before training started and crashed at my cousin's apartment in Beverly Hills for about a week. One day, after a hard day of work, my cousin came home and delicately told me, "Houseguests are like fresh fish. After a while, they start to stink." I knew it was time to find a new roommate, and fortunately, a friend of my cousin's was looking for one. I was too naive to realize that South Central wasn't exactly the best neighborhood in L.A., but a furnished place for $400 a month met my budget.

To this day, *having roommates has been the best financial decision I have ever made.* For my first six years out of college, I spent, on average, $300 less per month than if I had lived by myself. Three hundred dollars a month is $3,600 year. Stick with me here on the numbers for a second. Two thousand dollars of that $3,600 went into an IRA. Because an IRA is tax-deductible, I used the $500 in tax savings and the extra $1,600 to invest in a traditional brokerage account.

Six years later, the impact of that $300 per month savings was a whopping $62,000! Sure, the stock market did unusually well during those years, but had I not had those roommates, my money would have gone to my landlord and I would have missed out on those returns. When people ask me today, "How did you afford to live in a penthouse in Manhattan? How did you afford to travel around the world? Other than two years of your life, you have never made any real money," I tell them that having a roommate pays for a lot of trips to Bolivia. I also remind them that it's the everyday decisions that *seem* trivial that end up making the most significant impact on your financial health.

After four months in Los Angeles, living with my roommate in South Central, I went to Houston for TFA training and student-taught a kindergarten class in an underprivileged neighborhood. It did little to prepare me for my assignment as an eighth grade behavior disorder teacher in LaPlace, Louisiana, about thirty miles northwest of New Orleans. My role as a "baby-sitter" for sixteen-year-olds who barely read on a first-grade level and were often in trouble with the law made my job very difficult. One day, when I was in the heart of training for a marathon, one of my students purposely pushed a table over and broke my toe. Seeing a grown man brought to tears is not a pretty sight, even for the police who came to investigate.

Still, it was no excuse for quitting. To this day, *quitting my job as a teacher is the decision that I regret the most.* At the time, I rationalized it by saying that I wasn't helping anyway. In retrospect, I was just another in a long line of teachers who had given up on those kids and reinforced their own feelings of inadequacy. Quitting on myself is one thing—quitting on others is unacceptable.

Great guys that they are, my buddies wouldn't let me quit before Mardi Gras, and half a dozen or so flew in from all over the country to celebrate New Orleans–style. Of the group, three were in business school and two already had jobs on Wall Street. Listening to them spouting off about business made me realize how little I knew about personal finance. Suddenly, I had a plan: I still wanted to teach; I enjoyed finance; and I wanted to move out west. When I called Arizona State, I was thrilled that I hadn't missed the deadline to apply to their MBA program.

My decision to attend ASU in Tempe, Arizona, wasn't as random as it may have seemed. I wanted to learn more about finance, but I knew that taking on $75,000 worth of debt to go to a private business school was a quick path back to the trap. For the first time in my life, I took out a piece of paper and went through the process my mom called Q-Q-Kachoo and decided that I would attend only if I received a graduate assistantship (G.A.), which would give me free tuition and a small living stipend. Not only did I receive the assistantship, but I also was lucky enough to work for Dr. Donna Blancero—a dynamic professor who became an incredible mentor.

The summer before my first year at ASU, I went to Atlanta to work as a housing coordinator in the Olympic Village. After plunging toilets for world-class athletes and assembling beds for seven-footers Arvidas Sarbonis of Lithuania and Toni Kukoc of Croatia, I finally arrived at ASU in pursuit of my passion. I started writing a column about personal finance for the *MBA Newsletter* and devoted as much time to learning about personal finance as I did to my classes. I loved my job as a G.A., teaching college juniors who actually wanted to learn. I also set a goal of being published, which I accomplished on my first try. Granted, *Card Player* magazine isn't exactly *The Wall Street Journal*, but seeing my name in print was definitely a thrill.

I didn't even bother worrying about how I'd pay my living expenses. I reasoned that it wouldn't cost me much to live, and if I started to run short, I could always play poker on the Indian reservation that was only twenty minutes away. Remember when I talked about the impact of always having a roommate? As good a decision as that was, *not taking out low-interest student loans to pay expenses was the worst financial decision I have ever made.* Sure enough, I started to run short and my first trip to the reservation cost me eight hundred bucks. My second trip was worse. Instead of taking advantage of low-interest student loans, I started selling the stocks I had accumulated. Bear in mind, from 1996 to 1999, stocks went up more than they had in almost any time in history. Had I taken out loans instead of selling those stocks, my savings would have more than doubled.

By the end of my first year of business school, I was still in decent financial shape and any worries I had were more than offset by the news of my summer internship at a professional money management firm in San Diego. What I saw firsthand that summer was *why* even the pros have a tough time beating the stock market, which ultimately helped shape my investment philosophy. Don't get me wrong, the pros were brilliant men and women, but the stock market just isn't rational and it's all but impossible to outsmart. When the average person tries to beat it, and they have to pay for the salaries and fancy offices of these brokerage professionals, research has shown that eight times out of ten, it's a losing proposition.

With news of my internship, which added credibility to my burgeoning career in financial planning, I decided to cut a deal with Dr. Blancero. I told her that I would return as a G.A. under one condition: that I could give one lecture each semester on financial planning. It was an easy sell. The column I had been writing for the *MBA Newsletter* was so well received by my classmates that I was given the unofficial title of "Class Financial Planner." What amazed me was how little MBA students knew about their finances. If the future business leaders of America didn't know much about personal finance, I figured the average person was really in trouble. That's when I knew I had chosen a good career. There was no shortage of people who needed financial help, and knowing how much of an impact I could make got my blood pumping again.

On My Way Back to "the Trap"

Right before I left Arizona for the summer, I met a woman named Michelle. We immediately connected and kept in touch while I was in San Diego. When she came to visit for a weekend, I remember how impressed I was by her generosity. One time when we were "just window-shopping," she saw an antique pipe at a novelty shop and said, "I *have* to get that for Keisha!" and pulled some loose cash out of her back pocket without as much as a thought. When I wanted to take a nap, she decided to treat herself to a manicure and a pedicure. Michelle knew how to live life, and her happy-go-lucky attitude struck me.

When school started, Michelle wasn't so happy-go-lucky. With a two-year-old son, a full-time job, and a major in interior design, her schedule was enough to stress anyone out. With almost no money and a credit rating so bad that she couldn't even get a credit card, her anxiety level was off the charts. I wasn't surprised when she decided to get back together with her ex and have another child with him. She had always wanted a sibling for her son, and those feelings intensified when she suddenly lost her seventeen-year-old brother to meningitis at the beginning of her pregnancy.

Meanwhile, my financial situation was worsening by the day. After going through most of the money I had saved, I decided that the best way to compensate for not taking out student loans was to use low-interest credit cards. I reasoned that by paying 6.9 percent, I was getting a better rate with a credit card than if I had used student loans. Financially, it was a savvy move. The problem was that it became too easy to spend money. I started learning more about human nature.

The credit cards came in the mail faster than I could catch a last-minute flight to Vegas and book a suite at the Mirage. With graduation on the horizon and aspirations of becoming a financial therapist, I found myself back in "the trap." How did I let it happen—again?

With debt mounting, I had no choice but to give up on my dream of becoming a financial therapist. After deliberating over low-paying jobs that I was actually passionate about, I had no choice but to take the highest-paying job I was offered. I ended up working as a management consultant for Price Waterhouse in Chicago.

When I cashed my five-figure signing bonus, I had officially "sold out." Not that there is anything wrong with the profession of management consulting, it's just that I chose ASU so that financial considerations wouldn't rule my job search. Once again, I found myself chasing my bills and not my dreams. By August, I was shuttling back and forth between Chicago and Tampa, writing proposals and building PowerPoint slides—hardly inspiring stuff.

The summer before I started work, I treated myself to a little vacation. With a holster of low-interest credit cards strapped to my waist, I took off for Europe. One would have thought that a five-figure signing bonus would have covered my travels and then some, but it didn't come close. With all my credit cards, it became too easy to spend money. When I arrived back in Chicago, Michelle was in her eighth month of pregnancy and had broken up with her ex. As the expected baby's godfather, I knew I was taking on a lot of responsibility. But with Michelle's finances in disarray, I was counted on for more than just moral support.

That's when I knew I had to do something to get control of my financial situation. I was in real bad shape and I needed someone to talk to. Normally I would have turned to my parents, but my family thought I had bitten off more than I could chew. Instead, I decided to call my friend Darius, an investment manager on Wall Street who also happens to be one of my best friends and an incredibly objective decision maker. Soon, I was on my way to developing financial therapy. I started tutoring Michelle, and she started referring all of her friends to me. In no time, the Finance Doctor had a thriving practice.

8 Steps for Financial Wellness

Before we begin our therapy, I want you to ask yourself this one simple question: "If money weren't an issue, how would I be living my life?"

By the end of this book, you will have a solid plan so that your dreams, and not your bills, will drive the way you live your life. I can't promise that you will be able to attain Dr. Dink Utopia, but you will certainly have all the tools and knowledge to chart your course.

Financial therapy is intended to add a little structure to the common sense that you already have. What you learn won't impress you as much as the techniques that allow you to actually carry it out.

The 8 Steps are as follows:

1. Apply Q-Q-Kachoo to Decision Making
2. Create Your Vision of Financial Wellness
3. Use the Buyer's Antibiotic for Big Purchases
4. Enjoy the Money You Earn—Stop Giving It to the Banks
5. Monitor Your Vital Signs—Make More Than You Spend
6. Keep Your Balance and Know the Rule of 72
7. Understand the Risks and Rewards of Investing
8. Maintain Financial Wellness for a Lifetime

I do not see financial therapy as a means to an end. It may be a means to getting rich, but I have never associated money with happiness. I associate happiness with following your dreams. *My purpose in writing this book is to teach you how to prevent the worries of money from entering your thoughts so you can concentrate on the people you love and the activities you enjoy doing.*

At the end of each chapter, you will be asked to do a brief exercise. Please take the time to do it. It will be your way of taking the all-important steps towards financial wellness for a lifetime.

Preliminary Exercise

Put the book down and ask yourself the following questions:

1. Do you find yourself chasing your bills?
2. Are you doing the job you dreamed about as a kid?
3. Do you feel "trapped" because of mounting bills and excessive debt?
4. Do you have a plan that you are executing or are you just living day to day?
5. Do you ever wonder why it seems as though everyone is getting rich in the stock market, but you haven't taken the time to figure out how it all works?
6. Do you know the definition of a mutual fund, an IRA, and the Dow Jones?
7. How do you feel when you think about planning for education, buying a home, and living out your retirement?
8. Do you ever wonder why no one ever taught you all this stuff?
9. Finally, think about where it hurts now and why.

Chapter 1

Dr. Dink Is Born

The pattern of get up, go to work, pay bills, get up, go to work, pay bills . . . Their lives are forever run by two emotions, fear and greed. Offer them more money, and they continue the cycle by also increasing their spending. This is what I call the Rat Race.

—Robert T. Kiyosaki

Even though I go by "Dr. Dink," I didn't go to medical school and I don't know the difference between a thyroid and a fibroid. But I do know the difference between $25,000 worth of credit card debt and a lifetime of financial wellness. As you now know, I wasn't always the Finance Doctor. In fact, my own financial problems alerted me to just how hard it is to become financially healthy. But it was really my best friend Michelle's financial woes that gave me pause and forced me to come up with a viable form of financial therapy.

Michelle, in many ways, epitomizes the typical American. She has big dreams for herself—and even more so for her kids. She believes in education and is willing to go into debt to get it. She wants the world for her kids and will spare no expense when it comes to their health, education, and development. Like most of us, she dreams of being a homeowner, having passion for her career, and paying for her kids' education.

When I met Michelle, she was in her late twenties, broke, maxed out on her credit cards, and fighting to put herself through college. She was working three full-time jobs—parent, student, and interior designer—and never seemed to have enough hours in the day or greenbacks in her wallet. She was a fighter and a survivor, but even her best intentions could not prevent her from financial chaos. When it came to money, Michelle simply did not know better. She was not a compulsive shopper and she never put herself before her kids, but she simply ran out of money each month.

For all that is made in the media about the "me" generation, Michelle's financial problems were not the result of selfishness or irresponsibility. She simply lacked knowledge, which is no surprise, since financial education is not taught in school, and only given later in life to the rich who have the luxury of paying for financial advisors. What I didn't realize until I had known Michelle for almost a year is that when it comes to her money, she lived her life in denial. As my mom likes to say, "De-Nial is not just a river in Egypt."

Michelle made up her mind to be the best mother she could be and get a degree, and she wasn't going to let anything stop her. When she ran out of money, she did what most of us do—she borrowed. It started out with a small student loan, and before you knew it, Michelle had tapped every credit source she could. Credit cards and department store cards were her favorite poison, and she often paid interest rates as high as 22 percent—not that she was even paying attention. It wasn't as if she made a conscious decision to get into this mess. In fact, she did all she could not to think about money. She just figured that if she smothered her kids with love and dedicated herself to mastering interior design, things would somehow work themselves out. They did not.

When I first met Michelle, I was in business school and had really taken to teaching my friends about their finances. Michelle knew it was my passion, but never seemed to ask for any advice. She would come to my lectures for support, but would never go so far as to create her vision of financial wellness—something I ask my students to do right off the bat. When I would ask Michelle about her finances, her answer was always the same: "I don't want to talk about it. It just gives me a headache."

As I said, in many ways, Michelle epitomizes the typical American. Talking or thinking about our finances is depressing, and it's something that is just easier to avoid. When Michelle's phone got cut off, she shrugged it off and bought a prepaid phone card. When her electricity got turned off, she worked overtime on the weekend and paid the bill. But soon enough, it caught up to her. It always does.

My buddy Big Jim once told me, "If a person gets desperate enough, there isn't one thing that person wouldn't do for ten dollars." I disagreed and an argument ensued, but after giving it some thought, I realized that maybe Big Jim was right. The thought of the things that desperate people do for money makes me cringe. But Michelle is not most people. She is stubborn, she is proud, and she is a fighter. Stealing is not part of her character. Quitting isn't, either—especially when it comes to education. Going on welfare would never cross her mind, and asking a friend for a loan would be unthinkable. Then again, she never thought it could get this bad.

When she received the letter from her landlord stating that she would be evicted from her apartment if she didn't come up with $900 in three days, she had little choice but to go to her best friend—me. Michelle never has a problem expressing herself, but she could hardly get the words out. Before she asked me for the loan, I honestly thought she was going to tell me that somebody died.

Given the degree of emotion, my first thoughts were not Q-Q-Kachoo. I remember thinking that I was in a lose-lose situation. Lend her the money and not only would I put myself further in debt, but I also might jeopardize our friendship. Deny her the money and watch my best friend and her innocent two-year-old son get thrown out on the street. Just as my mom did when Andy went to her with his request to devote his entire summer to football, I stalled.

I spent a day or two thinking about Michelle's situation, and then I remembered what my mom would tell me over and over as a kid: "There is no trust fund. There is no family business to run. The only thing you can depend on is your education." Her wisdom was not lost on me. I knew that one way or another Michelle would land on her feet. I also knew that the only way she could do it was to drop out of school.

I try not to harp too much on the past, but I also strive never to make the same mistake twice. Quitting my job as a schoolteacher is still the decision I regret the most in my life. And while the situation was vastly different, the decision to further an individual's education rested in my hands.

My friend Jimmy, the one who likes to quote the Bible, also has an affinity for quoting Shakespeare. When I told him about my predicament, he cautiously reminded me, "Neither a borrower nor a lender be." My dad had told me the same thing when I was younger, and it had served me well—especially in my days as a poker player. I could see the wisdom in Jimmy and Dad's words, but this was my best friend we were talking about here. The question of the day became: How far do you actually go when you tell your best friend that you will "help" her get through college?

I did a quick Q-Q-Kachoo, and the numbers and the cons pointed to not lending her the money. But when I checked my gut, I knew that my decision had already been made. As it turned out, the amount of the loan wasn't as important as was the fact that it set a precedent. Michelle still had two years left of school and was about to give birth to my goddaughter, and her financial troubles were not going away. We halfheartedly worked out a budget and put together a plan to get Michelle through school, but every bill became an issue. Since I'm just as stubborn as Michelle, there was no way I was going to let her drop out of school. And as much as I tried not to let it, my relationship with Michelle was taking its toll on me, both financially and emotionally.

My friends and family contended that I had bitten off more

than I could chew, and they were right. Just after my goddaughter was born, I decided to get out of denial myself and saw that I was in $25,000 worth of credit card debt. At this point, I was out of business school and making good money as a management consultant, but I still didn't think that I could weather two more years of managing my own budget as well as Michelle's. Not surprisingly, it had also begun to put a strain on our friendship.

I've always trusted my parents' judgment, but in this instance, I felt they were too close to the situation. I asked some friends, and their opinions were unanimous. My buddy Spencer summed it up best: "Cut her off. You need to look after yourself." I was beginning to lose faith in the human spirit. Most of my friends had help paying for college, and several of my friends' parents had paid every cent. Still, not one suggested that I lend Michelle a hand. I wondered if all my friends had turned into greedy pigs or if they were just looking out for me. I suppose I was looking for a tender heart when I called my good friend Darius, an old college pal who was just starting to make a name for himself on Wall Street. It was that fateful conversation that changed my life, even my name.

"Darius," I said in a fit of panic, "I don't know what to do. I just started a new job in a new city. I'm $25,000 in debt, and Michelle's expenses are going up. I've talked to some other friends, and the consensus is now that she's had her baby, I need to be selfish and cut her off. What do you think?"

In his usual careful, objective manner, Darius answered, "I can tell you from my own experience that lending money almost always leads to hard feelings. But I don't know that much about Michelle's situation. How much school does she have left?"

"Two more years. Assuming she can even afford to stay in school," I said.

"You mean, assuming *you* can afford to keep her in school? And if you don't keep her in school, what are her options? Can she get help from her family or can she get student loans?"

"She's already defaulted on her student loans and her credit is so bad that she can't even get a credit card," I told Darius, while I instantly had a flashback to the time Michelle bought her friend Keisha that pipe in San Diego. "To answer your question," I continued, "if I don't help her with her expenses, she'll have to drop out of school."

"And if she drops out now," Darius finished my thought, "there's probably little chance she'll ever go back and get her degree. How old is she and how old are her kids?"

"She's twenty-nine, her son is three, and her daughter is two weeks old. I don't know how, but she was working and going to class right up until she gave birth, and she hasn't slowed down one bit since."

"Under most circumstances," Darius said, "I would tell you not to lend her money, because doing that usually leads to more trouble in the long run. But because Michelle is working hard in school and getting her degree is probably her only shot at ever becoming independent, I think you need to make sure she can afford to stay in school. I hate to use a cliché, but I think it holds true in this case: 'Give a man a fish, and he'll eat for a day; teach a man to fish, and he'll eat for a lifetime.' "

I thought of my friends Barry and Francis. Both were able to get into good colleges because I helped them prepare for the SAT. But neither of them got their degree, because I didn't teach them how to be better students. Darius was making a good point. He continued: "Obviously, you're not going to let your goddaughter go hungry. Plus, if you want to see Michelle become self-reliant, it all hinges on her getting a degree and finishing her education."

"I agree," I told Darius. "That's basically how I got into so much debt to begin with. But we're not talking about nickels and dimes here. I just feel like once again, I'm in a lose-lose situation. I simply can't help Michelle without hurting myself."

"I see your point," Darius said, "but let me ask you this: In thirty years, do you think you're going to look back and wish you had that extra money?"

"Of course not," I replied, "but you work on Wall Street, where it seems like they print money every day. It'd be different if I was lending her money that I already have, but the reality is that I'm paying Michelle's expenses with debt."

"I'm glad you brought up Wall Street," Darius said, "since her situation is very similar to what happens during an international financial crisis. Think about when a country has an economic problem—what does the United States government do?"

I wasn't in the mood for one of Darius's Wall Street analogies, so I gave him the answer I thought he was looking for: "They bail 'em out."

"Not quite," Darius replied. "Yes, the United States will often give economic aid, but it will come in the form of loans, and it will also include a program that teaches a country how to avoid future mistakes and how to lay the groundwork for a solid economy. If all goes well, the country will bounce back, which ultimately will help the United States as well."

"So what you're saying is that by helping Michelle through her crisis, it will ultimately be good for both of us. In other words, I should keep lending her money."

"You got the first part right—it will ultimately be good for the both of you," he said. "But I can't believe you're missing the main point! If your goal is to help Michelle become self-reliant, money is not the answer."

"Wait a second," I said, confused. "So now you're saying that I shouldn't lend her money."

"I guess I'm going to have to spell this out for you," Darius responded, sounding a little disappointed that I had missed the essence of his analogy. "Yes, you should continue to lend her money to help pay for her education. But, more important, you need to teach her *how to become financially independent.* You have an MBA, you've written articles and given speeches on personal finance, yet I haven't heard you say one thing about creating a plan for Michelle. What's missing from this picture is financial education."

"Michelle and I have talked about making a budget for her to follow, but neither one of us has followed through on the plan," I said, disgusted with myself.

Darius's usually deliberate words were suddenly filled with passion. "Forget about the money, your most valuable resource is what's in between your ears—your knowledge."

I agreed with Darius, but Michelle's situation seemed so urgent and so overwhelming that I really had no idea how to begin. I said, "Darius, I don't even know where to start. Should I just send her a budget?"

"You should be able to answer that better than I can. After working as a teacher and getting an MBA in finance, this should be your area of expertise. But I would like to remind you that one of your favorite sayings is 'Prescription without diagnosis is malpractice.'"

"What does that have to do with anything?" I asked. Darius is one of those guys who like to lead people to their own conclusions without imposing his own will, but for some reason, I'd lost his train of thought.

Always intuitive, he sensed my confusion and tried another approach. "Back when you were a salesman, you would always start your pitch by asking your prospects a bunch of questions. Then, based on a person's wants and needs, you would offer a solution. Why should Michelle's situation be any different? Instead of helping someone decide what kind of siding would be best for their home, you're helping Michelle decide what's best for her future."

Darius was definitely onto something, and I tried picking up where he left off. "First I need to ask Michelle questions, then we have to come up with a solution. But the solution can't be a one-shot deal. It needs to be a series of exercises that she can perform over the course of months. Eventually, she'll understand her financial situation, create a vision, and be on the road to financial wellness for a lifetime."

"It's very simple," Darius said, sensing my enthusiasm. "You ask a bunch of questions, come up with a diagnosis, begin treating the problems, and then outline a plan to keep the patient healthy. It sounds kind of like therapy."

"It *is* therapy. I love the idea, but I don't want to use the word *patient.* I don't see myself as someone who can fix a problem with some miracle solution. What I can do is teach people concepts so that they can fix the problems themselves."

"So, Dink," said Darius, calling me by the nickname that came from Dinkin, my last name, "if you are a teacher, call them students. Either way, you are providing financial therapy. And what better way than to start with your best friend. If all goes well, you will have made an impact on the future of four lives—Michelle's, her two kids', and most important, your own. You better get started, Mr. Finance Doctor. Or should I just call you Dr. Dink?"

From that day forward, I was known as Dr. Dink.

What Is Financial Therapy?

I did not hang up the phone with Darius and immediately come up with a foolproof plan for financial therapy. It was only after years of research, interviews, and trial and error that I was able to harness all my knowledge into an effective prescription. I was fortunate that I could learn from all the things my parents did right as well as all the things Michelle and I did wrong. Many people would contend that I have a lot of nerve creating financial therapy when I was in $25,000 worth of credit card debt myself. My buddy Richie once said to me, "Do you really think people want to learn from someone who has been on the couch himself?" The question forced me to reflect. Who was I to teach when I had made so many mistakes myself? What gives me a right to tell people to chase their dreams when I had sold out for money—not once, but twice?

After thinking it over, I realized that I am not perfect and I too am prone to human error. It's the nature of our species. I told Richie, "I do not tell my students, 'Do as I say,' nor do I tell them,

'Do as I do.' I simply share my knowledge and stories and provide a prescription. I am able to understand my students because I, too, had been in a situation where I cringed every time I got my credit card bills in the mail. It's not the fact that I had fallen into the trap twice, but the fact that I got out of the trap twice."

For those who have a desire to learn and change, financial therapy has proven to be effective. That does not mean that I have all the answers or any miracle cures. Knowledge without a change in behavior is equivalent to ignorance. And as I have slowly started to accept, changing behavior goes against not only human nature, but also physics. Just as an object in motion tends to stay in motion and an object at rest tends to stay at rest, a student who is financially unhealthy, even with good intentions, tends to stay financially unhealthy. But just because it's difficult doesn't mean it's impossible. Michelle and I were both able to overcome this natural tendency and are currently chasing our dreams. With a dose of common sense, motivation, and education, you can be on your way as well.

The 8 Steps for Financial Wellness are an extension of common sense, education, and my life's experiences. My personal struggles and Michelle's stubbornness forced me to create a plan that was easy to carry out. All the genius in the world is a waste if it can't be applied. I took the KISS principle to heart: Keep It Simple, Stupid.

Asking students to write down every single expense or to create intricate spreadsheets wasn't going to work. Telling my students never to indulge themselves would only lead to binge spending. Demanding that they sacrifice life's material pleasures goes against my personal belief that, as Natalie Merchant of 10,000 Maniacs so beautifully sings, "These Are the Days."

I threw the "kitchen sink" at Michelle as my first test student; some things worked and some things did not. Working with Michelle was kind of like tossing a yo-yo while going up an escalator. There were constant ups and downs, but the trend was always moving upward. As I taught Michelle everything I knew about personal finance, I also applied the knowledge to my own life as well.

I know this sounds far-fetched, but by applying my own 8-step prescription, I was able to eliminate all $25,000 of my credit card debt in less than a year and a half and still max out my 401(k) plan.

Throughout that period of time, I shared my ideas with family and friends and counseled anyone who would listen. The most consistent feedback that I received from my students was to *keep things simple.* Every time I tried to apply the fancy concepts I learned in business school or as a consultant, my students would tune me out. When I used words like *debits, credits,* and *income statements,* all I got were a bunch of blank stares.

I knew that I had to put all of my materials together to create a prescription that would work for people. My challenge was to keep things interesting and still not leave out any of the essentials. Eventually, I came up with the following prescription for financial wellness.

An 8-Step Prescription for Financial Wellness

Most people who get an MBA in finance are sticklers for details and are bean counters. Cutting corners can be a great skill for a businessperson, but it's never been my speed. I prefer to round off. I can't dispute "a penny saved is a penny earned," but I just don't think it's much fun going through life pinching pennies. I put my stock in another cliché: "don't be penny-wise and pound-foolish." In other words, concentrate on the big decisions in life and, to steal a phrase, don't sweat the small stuff. Perhaps that is why I spend so much time talking about my mom's formula, Q-Q-Kachoo.

I learned that being too rigid and worrying about each and every bill just isn't sustainable. It's like a crash diet—it will work for a couple of days, but at some point, you'll get so sick of denying yourself that you'll spend the next four days eating nothing but Twinkies and Ho-Hos. With this in mind, I put together a prescription that focuses on the big picture.

1. Apply Q-Q-Kachoo to Decision Making

When it comes to big decisions in life, use this three-step process. The first Q stands for Quantitative—do the numbers. The second Q stands for Qualitative—do a Ben Franklin by listing the pros and cons. The Kachoo reminds you to check your gut.

2. Create Your Vision of Financial Wellness

Many of us are so programmed to go through the motions and pay the bills that we forget to dream. I cannot begin to express how important it is to create a vision. Therefore, I'll leave it to three others:

> We write our own destiny; we become what we do.
> —Chiang Kai-shek

> The future belongs to those who prepare for it.
> —Ralph Waldo Emerson

> Futures don't just happen . . . they are created.
> —Anonymous

3. Use the Buyer's Antibiotic for Big Purchases

From clothes to gifts to vacations to lawn mowers to houses to cars, we are constantly buying things. In order to get good value and get the most out of those purchases, my brother, Andy, and I created the Buyer's Antibiotic, which will allow you to beat salespeople at their own game.

4. Enjoy the Money You Earn—Stop Giving It to the Banks

So much of our budget seems to go to interest and fees, especially to credit card companies. By following some simple suggestions, you can learn how to put that money toward things you enjoy instead of making the banks rich.

5. Monitor Your Vital Signs—Make More Than You Spend

This step is the easiest to understand, but the most difficult to execute. Good financial health starts with making more than you spend every month. With the help of an expert, my mom, you will learn creative ways to balance your monthly budget.

6. Keep Your Balance and Know the Rule of 72

I do my best to stay away from accounting. That's why I use simple language to show you how to create your own balance sheet so you know exactly where you stand. The Rule of 72 teaches you how to double your money, hopefully every six years, by taking advantage of compound interest.

7. Understand the Risks and Rewards of Investing

In an era of high-flying Internet stocks, we often lose sight of the fact that there are no "free lunches" in the world of investing. As someone who's about to take control of their financial life, it's crucial that you know the basics of investing, managing risk, and setting realistic expectations.

8. Maintain Financial Wellness for a Lifetime

As the saying often goes, the hard part isn't getting there, it's staying there. By dedicating no more than a half hour each month and an extra half hour every six months, you can turn your dire financial health into financial wellness for a lifetime.

Now that you know my prescription, you can see that it is very basic. In fact, some of my friends were a little critical of my prescription when they first saw it. They were disappointed that it didn't include any get-rich-quick schemes or miracle cures. I explained that my prescription is based on the fact that *people know what to do.* All you need is a little bit of common sense to identify a problem. The challenge is *how to actually do it.* Even I, the self-proclaimed Finance Doctor, made enough bad decisions to put myself in the trap—twice. It wasn't until I perfected all 8 Steps that I was able to create the right prescription.

Michelle encouraged me to pursue teaching financial wellness as a career. She argued that since I was finally out of debt, I had no excuse not to follow my dream. Plus, she had already found me two students—a couple named Cindy and Scott. I told Michelle to have them attend a lecture I was giving on the campus at Arizona State University, and if they liked what I had to say, they should approach me after the lecture and introduce themselves.

I tried to get some information about this couple, but Michelle didn't know much. All she told me was that Cindy seemed very stressed about her finances and the two of them often commiserated about how tough it is to make ends meet. Michelle told me that the couple had grown so desperate that they even put $300 into a pyramid scheme—and, of course, never saw the money again.

After some more probing, I learned that Cindy and Scott have a combined net income of about $36,000, rent a modest town house, and have two young kids. And although Michelle couldn't offer any specifics, she did tell me that Cindy often complained about being a prisoner to her credit cards. As much as I stress the importance of forming an individual diagnosis, I find many similarities in the problems most of my students face. Thus, I had a pretty good idea what to expect from Cindy and Scott. Most people come to me to learn how to get out of debt, how to save enough money for a house, how to invest, and how to stop feeling so powerless over their finances.

I had Michelle give Cindy and Scott their first set of exercises to complete before they attended the lecture. Like it or not, changing behavior is not a passive process, and I wanted them to be involved from the start. The first exercise is very simple.

Exercise 1

Think about and make a list of five important decisions you will have to make over the next five years. This list may include paying for your child's or your own education, buying or leasing a car, and buying a home.

1.

2.

3.

4.

5.

Chapter 2

Apply Q-Q-Kachoo to Decision Making

What ultimately determines who we become and where we go in life? The answer is our decisions. It's in these moments that our destiny is shaped.

—Anthony Robbins

Michelle called to tell me that Cindy and Scott would be attending the lecture and were excited to get started. The timing couldn't have been better, as Dr. Blancero had asked me to give her students a speech on the importance of sound decision making. Financial therapy starts with making good decisions, and it's no coincidence that I start by teaching Q-Q-Kachoo.

Addressing six hundred students, in addition to Cindy and Scott, I shook off my nerves and said, "The process for you to decide whether or not you want to attend graduate school is the same process that General Motors uses to decide if it should invest in a new factory. As business students, you spend so much time dissecting big corporations and discussing their decisions. You look at financial statements, analyze the company's mission and goals, and evaluate all the alternatives before making a decision. What I think you often fail to do is use that same analytical process to make decisions for yourself. After all, it is much easier to make decisions for a company or for a friend, but when it comes to personal decisions, you can't help but let your emotions get involved. And as you all have learned, emotions are often the enemy of sound decision making."

It seemed as though I had the students' attention, and I wanted to keep it by getting them involved. "Before we talk about graduate school and the time and money involved, are there any other major purchases that you are contemplating? And don't worry about raising your hand—just call out."

"I'm trying to decide if I should buy or lease a car," a young woman named Brooke called out. "I've never really heard a straight answer on which one is really better."

Fortunately, I had an example prepared and was ready to run with it. I was a little concerned that I might lose the students by being overly detailed, but I wanted to be sure that they understood the whole process. For most decisions, the financial impact is not a one-shot deal, but rather it's one that's realized over a number of years. I said to the students, "For a car, what I like to do is look at the cost over a six-year period. It's human nature to want to pay the least possible amount up front, but paying less up front often means paying more in the end. In general, a lease can be tempting because the monthly payments are often lower than if you buy."

"Lower monthly payments?" Brooke asked. "Well, case closed, then. The lease must be better."

Brooke's comment frustrated me, since her mentality is the same mentality of most consumers. Very few take the time to think about the *total* cost and simply try to get the best car with the lowest monthly payments. Rather than show my frustration, I told the students, "That's not necessarily so. You have to do a fair amount of homework before making this decision. You can get a good idea of a car's current value and resale value by picking up the *Blue Book* or doing research on the Internet. In terms of financing, you can check interest rates in the newspaper or from your bank. Another thing to consider is buying a car with cash."

"Sorry, Dr. Dink, but the cash tree in my backyard burned down a long time ago," Brooke said, sounding frighteningly like my mom.

Even though I know most college students—or most *people,* for that matter—don't have enough cash to buy a car, I can never resist the urge to teach a quick lesson, so I said to Brooke, "Pretend for a second that you have fifteen grand in cash. You now have to decide whether or not to pay cash for the car or finance it at 8.5 percent and invest the difference."

"Eight point five percent interest is cheap," said Brooke. "I'm sure I can do better than that in the stock market. A lot of those Internet stocks have gone up 300 percent in just a few months."

I might have thought her comment was funny if I hadn't encountered so many others who held unrealistic expectations about the stock market. But I decided to use logic to appeal to Brooke and her classmates and said, "Paying interest is money that goes right out of your pocket and into the pocket of a banker. You might be able to offset that interest by investing, but more often than not, *avoiding debt is one of the best investments you can make.*"

I was sure many of the students brushed this comment off. After all, it's so much sexier to talk about what stocks you are buying and how cool you are because you have a broker. But for those in the know, *avoiding high-interest debt is the first step in accumulating wealth.* I knew I was getting a bit sidetracked, so I got back to the topic at hand by saying, "From a pure financial perspective, it usually makes more sense to buy a car rather than lease."

"But, Doc, there are so many things to consider," said Brooke. "First of all, I don't know how long I want to keep a car. Second of all, I don't want to go through the hassle of selling the car when the time comes. And you can talk about 'average' maintenance costs until you're blue in the face, but there's always a chance that something could break that would cost thousands of dollars. The only bad thing about a lease is that I don't know how many miles I'll drive the car and I worry about having to pay a penalty since most leases set the number of miles you're allowed to drive in a given year. So, what do you think I should do?"

I was not about to answer that question for her. With a small dose of Q-Q-Kachoo, I was confident that Brooke could reach her own conclusions. At this point in the lecture, I hadn't even mentioned the magic formula, but I decided to flash an example that I had created up on the board so we could walk through it. I said to the class, "This is a real case study of my roommate's decision when he was looking to get a new car. Here are the assumptions."

- The car sells for $18,343. The interest rate is 8.55 percent.
- The up-front costs, including taxes and fees, are $1,834 in order to purchase or lease.
- Using a six-year car loan, the monthly payments to purchase are $323/month ($3,876/year).
- Maintenance and upkeep will cost, on average, $50/month more for a purchased car than for a leased car ($600/year).
- To lease the same car using a thirty-six-month lease, the monthly payments are $311/month ($3,737/year).

The chart shows the cost in years one through six. For the purchased car, the inception cost is a one-time occurrence. For the leased car, there is an inception cost in year one, and again in year four, when a new lease is taken on. Think of the inception cost as your out-of-pocket expense to drive the car off the lot.

After I gave the students a chance to look over the numbers, I asked Brooke if her analysis was now complete. "Sure it is," she said. "The numbers always tell the story."

This was exactly the type of response I was expecting. For most people, looking at the numbers is the first—and sometimes the only—part of making a big decision. But as you now know, there is more to a financial decision than just analyzing the numbers. I smiled at Brooke, shook my head in disagreement, and calmly stated, "You know, Brooke, Ben Franklin would beg to differ."

Purchase Car							
Year	**1**	**2**	**3**	**4**	**5**	**6**	**Resale**
Inception cost	$1,834						$7,690
Total of payments	$3,876	$3,876	$3,876	$3,876	$3,876	$3,876	
Maintenance	$600	$600	$600	$600	$600	$600	
Lease Car							
Inception cost	$1,834			$1,834			
Total of payments	$3,737	$3,737	$3,737	$3,737	$3,737	$3,737	$0
To Purchase							
Total cost over six years: $28,690 – resale of $7,690 = $21,000, or $292/month							
To Lease							
Total cost over six years: $26,090, or $362/month							

The rest of the class looked at me like I was crazy and the look on their faces seemed to say, "What the heck does Ben Franklin have to do with buying a car?" Just as my mom had explained to me, I replied, "Whenever Ben had to make an important decision, he would take out a piece of parchment and draw a line down the middle. On one side he wrote the pros, and on the other side he wrote the cons. He then listed all the factors that went into making his decision."

I grabbed a Magic Marker, walked over to the dry erase board, and said to the class, "Let's do a quick Ben Franklin on buying versus leasing a car. You all do the talking and I'll do the writing."

After writing down what the students called out, the list looked like this:

Pros of Buying

Lower overall cost
No mileage requirements
The car is yours

Pros of Leasing

Lower monthly payments
Can get a new car every two or three years
Less hassle

Cons of Buying

Hassle of selling your car
Higher monthly cost
Unforeseen maintenance expenses

Cons of Leasing

Higher overall cost
Additional cost for extra mileage
No car at the end of the lease term

"Now that we have all that information, what do you think I should do, Dr. Dink?" asked Brooke.

I make it a rule not to tell my students what I think they should do, so that I don't lose sight of my goal—to teach them how to continually make good decisions. I tried to handle the question diplomatically and said, "I'm here to give you the tools to make good decisions, not to give you answers. But if you are pressing me for one, I would recommend that you keep your current car as long as possible. The cost of a car—new or leased—is tremendous, especially if you are in debt. For one, you probably won't get a very good interest rate on a loan. And two, the car payment will prevent you from paying off your high-interest loans. In fact, if it was at all possible, I would recommend getting rid of your car."

"Are you kidding me?" Brooke said. "There's no public transportation where I live, and I need my car to get back and forth from school and work."

She hit all the right notes. "Those are two of my favorite words," I told her. "*Public transportation.* I'm not suggesting that you sell your car now, but just understand the true expense of a car. When you add up the cost of the car, insurance, gas, maintenance, repairs, parking, and every other factor, it's absolutely incredible."

I knew that I had exaggerated the car example, but from personal experience—between buying a Camry with no money down and almost buying a Porsche—I had started to believe that cars were nothing more than a one-way ticket to the trap. I wanted to be sure the class had a firm grasp on the buying-versus-leasing decision, and when I asked Brooke to do the last step of the decision-making process—the gut check—she responded, "My gut tells me to put off getting a car as long as I can. Since I'm not much for haggling and I like having a new car, my instincts tell me to lease, but only when I have paid off my credit cards and saved up some cash."

Brooke's response led me to believe that she understood the process, but I still couldn't resist one last comment. "If you're going to get a car, strongly consider buying it used. We all love that new-car smell, but it will cost you a pretty penny. You've probably heard this a million times, but the minute you drive off that lot, your new car depreciates by 15 percent. My dad has never bought new, and neither have I."

I still hadn't even mentioned the term "Q-Q-Kachoo," and although the students probably thought I was speaking off the top of my head, I had actually walked them through the entire process. Using a mysterious voice, I said to the class, "Congratulations, you have just uncovered the magical formula known as Q-Q-Kachoo."

"What?" a student called out.

"Q-Q-Kachoo," I said. "Kachoo is my code word for doing a gut check. The three-step formula for decision making should be very easy to remember, especially since we just walked through it. The first Q stands for Quantitative—doing the numbers. The second Q stands for Qualitative—doing a Ben Franklin by listing the pros and cons. And the Kachoo reminds you to check your gut. It's a simple formula that has served me and my students well over the years."

Almost on cue, Brooke became my biggest cheerleader. "I can see how all three steps together can make the decision process an easy one. Just make sure that you always go through *all three steps* of the decision-making process. Always do a Q-Q-Kachoo."

Education

"I want help making my decision about going to graduate school," a young man named Joey called out from the front row. "That's what I came to learn about, especially since investing time and money in furthering one's education is a lot more complicated than buying or leasing a new car."

I was glad that Cindy and Scott—my new students—were there for this example. For just about everyone I meet, whether it's a parent thinking about their kids or a twenty-something thinking about graduate school, education is always a hot topic. And it doesn't apply just to college. Michelle went through this analysis when she was deciding if her son, Logan, should go to kindergarten at a public or private school. It's a decision that she will probably contemplate each and every school year, and it's a tough one since there is no real way to measure the true financial impact.

Some of my students don't always understand what I mean when I say "do the numbers." For Michelle's decision, the numbers meant more than figuring out the cost of private school. It also meant subtracting the savings in day care by sending Logan to a school that keeps him there longer than public school, as well as her savings in transportation costs because the private school happens to be right next to her office. Doing numbers isn't necessarily difficult, but it does require you to factor in all related costs and all related benefits.

I addressed Joey, "You have the tools to make this decision yourself, but because the ramifications of going to graduate school are a bit more involved, we'll walk through the process together. We will first have to make a ton of assumptions. Remember, your analysis is only as good as the assumptions you make."

"I'm a senior, so I've already done some homework," said Joey. "Going full-time, it will take three years to finish, and the cost, including all books, fees, and tuition, is $15,000 per year. I think I can get a student loan for 9 percent interest. That should cover the assumptions."

This was such a typical answer. Everyone always thinks doing their research means figuring out the costs—but it's just as important, if not more important, to think about the payback. I challenged Joey, "That covers the costs, but it tells me nothing about the benefits. I assume that the degree will allow you to earn more money once you graduate, but we need to have an idea of how much. Plus, you didn't even mention living expenses."

"I hadn't thought about all that stuff," said Joey. "How do I go about getting that information?"

"I would start by going to professionals in your field and asking them. I would also talk to recent graduates of that school and find out what kind of pay they received upon graduation. The Career Office at ASU or the school you are applying to should also be able to give you statistics on job placement and compensation. If you don't know what's in store for you after you graduate, you have to ask yourself why you are going back to school in the first place. What other questions should you be asking before you make your decision?"

"For one, I would want to know something about the job market," yelled out a student who was seated near the back of the room. "If the job market goes sour in three years, who's to say that you will earn more money because you have a graduate degree? Heck, who knows if you will even be able to get a job."

"Those are two excellent points," I said, "which is why you want to be realistic when you make your assumptions. The difference between a 5 percent pay increase and a 15 percent increase may be the deciding factor. Just make sure you do enough research that your assumptions are practical."

"I understand the process of doing the numbers," said Joey, "but it raises even more questions. Should you show an increase in salary for the first few years or for your entire career?"

"It's up to you to make the assumptions," I said. "Ask yourself if your income ten years from now will be a function of your performance on the job or the fact that you have a graduate degree."

"Both," called out a bunch of students.

I could see that the students wanted more answers and were waiting for me to fill in the blanks—something I couldn't do for every student in the room. I decided, instead, to offer general advice: "Just remember that figures don't lie but liars figure. If you wanted to build a case for going back to school, you could plug in the numbers and make it look good, but you would only be kidding yourself. Unfortunately, there is no rule of thumb that can take the place of you doing your own research. For a decision such as graduate school, I can't tell you if it's a good investment without knowing your field, where you intend to go to school, the job market, and your work ethic, among other factors. But once you make the assumptions, the formula is the same for doing the numbers—just add up the inflows and subtract the outflows."

I knew the class, as business students, understood what I meant when I said "inflows and outflows," but I hoped that Cindy and Scott understood as well. Outflows are the money that goes out of your pocket. As I showed in the car example, outflows are nothing more than the money you spend. When it comes to an investment—as opposed to an expense—it is important to consider the inflows as well. Inflows are the money that comes into your pocket—the fruits of your labor, so to speak. In the example of purchasing a car, the only inflow was the car's resale.

Drawing on this thought, I said to the class, "It's very important for you to distinguish between an expense and an investment, and it's not always clear-cut. Typically, a car is viewed as an expense, but if you are in a profession, such as real estate, where you have to drive your clients around, a car is also an investment. The same can be said for clothing, since the way you present yourself often leads to opportunities. On the flip side, going to graduate school just to kill time is not really an investment. Unless you can point to a return on investment, whether it be financial or spiritual, you have to view spending as an expense."

While I knew I didn't have time to expand on this thought, it stayed in my mind. It's so easy to look at every expense as an investment since all the marketers tell you that by spending money, you are investing in yourself. Whether it's a massage, a vacation, a pair of shoes, a mattress, or an antique, it seems that every expense out there is marketed as an investment. And to be fair, many are. If a weekly massage or a firm mattress increases your productivity, then you can certainly call it an investment. I just find that most of my students overspend and then try to justify it as an investment. And when that investment carries the burden of credit card interest, it can really become detrimental.

I wanted to get back to the graduate school example, so I grabbed a marker and said, "There is no way we can run the numbers for each of you, since you will all have different assumptions. What we can do is a Ben Franklin. I'll write and you all just call out."

Pros	**Cons**
Be happier and more fulfilled	Stress
Opens up doors personally	Might hurt family life
Opens up doors professionally	Hurts performance of current job
Could help social life	Could hurt social life
Big upside for future income	Anxiety of having more debt

After writing down the pros and cons, it was now time to do a Kachoo. I knew the students were looking for an answer—students always want answers—but for this decision, they would be on their own. I tried to get them to think and said, "The reason I can't tell you if it's a good idea to go to graduate school is that the answer is going to be different for every one of you. You need to think long and hard about how this decision is going to make you feel."

Apparently, Joey already had. "In my gut, I know I want to be an architect and I want the best education possible. But emotionally, I don't deal with debt very well. I think I would feel best if I went to work right after college, put away some money, and started taking classes at night. Then, if I felt comfortable enough financially, I could always leave my job and go full-time."

The class seemed impressed by Joey's analysis. So many times, we get wrapped up in the numbers that we forget about how we feel. In Joey's case, he didn't even have to figure out the numbers before coming to a decision that he felt comfortable with. Sensing that the students were enjoying Q-Q-Kachoo, I decided to build on the first two examples.

Buying a House

"What other major purchases are you pondering?" I asked the class.

"I'm thinking about buying a house," a young man named Jason called out. "And I'm actually in the market, so I'd like you to be very detailed in your analysis."

"I shouldn't have to be detailed," I said. "It's the same technique as the other examples. The only person who can do a detailed Q-Q-Kachoo is you. After all, it's your decision."

Jason seemed a bit humbled, but I picked him right back up when I said, "Let's walk through the numbers anyway. It's important that you consider all the factors: mortgage, property taxes, assessments or condo fees, homeowner's association fees, mortgage insurance, as well as the tax implications. Also, you need to think about the opportunity cost of a down payment—which means that if you put $10,000 down on a house, you are missing out on the opportunity to invest that money elsewhere. Finally, you'll need to consider appreciation of your property."

Jason seemed a little overwhelmed with all the details I threw at him, and asked, "As a rule of thumb, how much does a house cost with a thirty-year mortgage?"

"That depends on interest rates," I said, "but right now, a good rule of thumb, if interest rates are around 8 percent, is that a thirty-year mortgage is about seventy dollars for every $10,000 that the house costs." I knew that Jason was pulling me deep into the numbers, and I didn't want to get too sidetracked. A mortgage, first of all, is nothing more than a loan used to finance a house. And because there are so many different types of mortgages, I had to make sure that I spoke in general terms with the students.

Jason would have none of it, and he said, "So in other words, a house that costs a hundred grand would be about $700 a month. That's $200 less than my current rent. Sign me up."

"First of all," I answered, "a *better* rule of thumb that factors in all of the costs of buying a house is one hundred bucks per ten thousand," I said. "That $100,000 home will mean a monthly payment of more like $1,000. Let's look at the numbers first and then we'll discuss it more in detail."

Dr. Blancero flashed the following example up on the screen.

Buying a House That Costs $105,263	
Down payment of 5%	$5,263 (up-front cost)
Mortgage for $100,000 (thirty-year fixed rate of 8%, plus closing costs of $1,200)	$725 (monthly cost)
Personal mortgage insurance (PMI)	$90 (monthly cost)
Property taxes (1% of home's value)	$87 (monthly cost)
Homeowner's insurance	$38 (monthly cost)
Association or condo fees	$60 (monthly cost)
Total Monthly Cost	*$1,000*
Approximate monthly tax savings ($700 x .25)	$(175)
Cost w/tax savings	***$825***
Current rent	***$900***
Net savings—monthly	**$75**

I could tell from the audience that the students seemed encouraged by these numbers. While it's tough to find a home for a hundred grand, I wanted to use this example because it makes it easy to work with the math. If you are looking at a house that costs about $300,000, just triple the numbers in the chart. In other words, the total monthly cost would be about $3,000 a month.

Owning a home is such a common dream, and for the average person it is very attainable. The main reason is that the government helps homeowners. I suppose they feel it is good for society when people own their own homes. At a minimum, it promotes stability and helps to build communities, and thus the government provides two very strong financial incentives. The first is the availability of mortgages. Through programs such as the Federal Housing Authority (FHA) and Fannie Mae, the government especially helps first-time home buyers subsidize their mortgages.

In the old days, it was standard practice to put 20 percent down on a house. But nowadays, my friend Dirk, who is a mortgage broker, tells me that most people put down 5 percent and some even put nothing down. I tried to pass on some of his wisdom and said to the class, "My friend told me that selling mortgages is a piece of cake. When he shows people that their monthly payments sometimes go down when they own, renters become owners in a hurry."

"So why would anyone rent?" asked Jason.

This was a common question, and I answered it with my standard reply. "I can't speak for everyone, but I can certainly speak for myself. I don't own a home because I move around a lot and there are costs every time you buy and sell a home. The two things that I miss out on are a tax write-off and the chance to build equity in a home."

That brought me to the second financial incentive that the government gives people. I explained to the class, "The interest on your mortgage payments is tax-deductible. You also get to deduct your property taxes, so in the earlier example, you will be able to write off approximately $700 per month on your taxes. Over the course of a year, assuming a tax rate of 25 percent, you will be saving $2,100 on taxes."

"There are still a few things I don't understand," said Jason. "First of all, what is mortgage insurance?"

"Typically, if you can't afford to put 20 percent down, which most people can't do, then you have to pay mortgage insurance," I said. "But guys like my friend Dirk can help you avoid that through creative financing. There are even ways that you can put 5 percent down and avoid the mortgage insurance. Selecting a mortgage can be complicated, and there is no way I can explain all of the nuances right now. If nothing else, get at least three quotes and deal with someone you trust."

Jason acted as if I were the first one who had ever given him a straight answer on this stuff, and asked, "I also didn't quite get the whole tax write-off thing."

"The government gives you a tax incentive to buy a house," I said. "You get to deduct the interest payments from your mortgage as well as your property taxes against your income, which means you save additional money on your taxes."

"Doc, it looks like a no-brainer to buy," said Jason. "I didn't know it was this easy. Where do I sign up for the mortgage?"

"You don't exactly sign up," I said. "You have to get approved first, and the first thing you should do is call some lenders, either your bank or a mortgage broker, to see where you stand. There are so many different types of loans that your head will spin. What I will give you are some guidelines." On cue, Dr. Blancero flashed my notes on the screen.

Guidelines to Obtaining a Mortgage

- Meet with a lender (credit union, your bank, mortgage banker) to see how much you can afford.
- Research areas where you would like to live.

- Be sure to find out all the costs incorporated with the house, including property taxes, assessments, homeowner's fees, maintenance, trash removal, and so on.
- Get at least three bids on mortgages.
- Compare the cost of a house to the cost to rent; be sure to factor in taxes.

"Can't a real estate agent do all that for me?" asked Jason.

"Yes, but typically real estate agents help you find a house and then refer you to lenders," I said. "Don't make the mistake of taking only one bid just because your real estate agent is friends with the lender. Something a good agent will do is to make sure you know how expensive a house you can afford before he or she takes you to look at houses. There's no sense finding your dream home if you can't afford it."

"How do they determine what you can afford?" asked Jason.

"It's pretty simple," I said as I was starting to get a little worn down from all the questions. Instead of getting irritated, I decided to ask a few myself and said, "Jason, if you were going to give somebody a loan, what information would you want?"

"I'd want to know if they ever stiffed somebody before," he answered.

"Yes. That's called credit history. What else?"

"How much debt they have and how much they make," said Jason. "Oh, and also what they could put up for collateral."

"You're on the right track, Jason, and it's great to see you are so excited," I said as I was beginning to run out of juice. Luckily, Dr. Blancero had begun to make her way to the podium, and I decided to conclude with one of my favorite quotes from Frederick Wilcox. In my most important voice, I said to the class, "Remember that 'progress always involves risks. You can't steal second and keep your foot on first.'" With that, Dr. Blancero stepped up to the podium, took the microphone from me, and told the class that they were out of time. She then encouraged the students to e-mail me.

She knew from experience that I was always good at getting back to people.

Unlike Cindy and Scott, who would be going through the next seven steps of financial therapy, at least these students had the foundation to be financially healthy. After all, good financial health starts with making good decisions.

Preparing for Next Week

I started packing up my gear, and just before I was ready to head to the bus stop, Cindy and Scott approached me. They told me that they had done their first exercise and had learned a lot from the lecture. They seemed sincere and, like most students, a little bit intimidated. Just about every student I meet has a fear of looking dumb, and they all seem to think that they are the only ones who are ignorant on the topic of finance. It's my job to exhibit good "bedside manner" and put them at ease.

After answering some of their questions, I said, "The fact that you did the first exercise and came here today shows me that you are committed to learning, and I applaud that." Like most new students, they were excited to learn, and I knew now was the time to ask them to perform the most difficult exercise. I handed them two pieces of paper and said, "This series of exercises is like drawing blood. You're going to cringe at the thought of it, but it will only hurt for a second. When it's over, and I see the results, I can diagnose the problem and you will be on your way to getting better."

Without even looking at what I handed her, Cindy put the exercises in her briefcase and said as she left, "I guess it's time for us to stick out our tongues and say 'aaaaaaahh.'"

We made plans to meet at my favorite coffeehouse, Java Road, just three days later. I knew that the meeting would be rough, since students often feel hopeless when reality stares them in the face. Still, it was critical to find out where they stood, and I had created two forms to make it as painless as possible. If they actually took the time to do these exercises, I knew they would be off to a great start.

When I finally got on the bus and had a chance to reflect on the lecture, I was pleased with the results. I knew that some of the students who just wanted the answers may have left frustrated, but I did my best to show them that for big decisions, there is no simple formula. At least they learned that doing the numbers, consulting Ben Franklin, and doing a gut check are a great start for any big decision. Long live Q-Q-Kachoo!

Exercise 2
The Diagnosis

If we had more money, we would spend it on . . .

If we didn't have to work, we would spend our time . . .

Where does it hurt now?

What would make you feel better?

Are you taking any "medicine"? In other words, are you doing anything that will help you on the road to financial wellness?

At the end of financial therapy, we hope to . . .

Monthly Vital Signs

The most important element in your financial health is making more than you spend every month—that's why I call the monthly budget the Vital Signs. I have broken the Vital Signs down into four categories. The first is the inflows—money coming in—such as your monthly paycheck. The last three categories are outflows and are divided as such: What's Going Out—Before You Get Out of Bed; What's Going Out—Basic Necessities; and What's Going Out—If You Had to Live Without. Fill in the blanks as accurately as you can.

Monthly Vital Signs	
What's Coming In	
Take-home pay from primary jobs	
Other income	
TOTAL INFLOWS	
What's Going Out—Before We Get Out of Bed	
Rent/mortgage	
Basic utilities—electricity, gas, water, basic phone	
Renter's/homeowner's insurance	
Car insurance—car 1	
Car insurance—car 2	
Life insurance (do not add if already taken out of take-home pay)	
Additional medical insurance, including dental	
Car payment 1	
Car payment 2	
Other monthly payments	
Credit card payments	
Student loans	
TOTAL WHAT'S GOING OUT—BEFORE WE GET OUT OF BED	
What's Going Out—Basic Necessities	
Groceries—in-home eating	
Basic clothing	
Gas and car maintenance	
Child care	
Other—dry cleaning, laundry, cleaning supplies, etc.	
Pet-related expenses	
TOTAL WHAT'S GOING OUT—BASIC NECESSITIES	
What's Going Out—If You Had to Live Without	
Long-distance phone	
Cable, basic and additional movie channels	
Clothes and other shopping goodies	
Toys, videos, music	
Eating out	
Cell phones	
Household services—cleaning, lawn care	
TOTAL WHAT'S GOING OUT—IF YOU HAD TO LIVE WITHOUT	

Chapter 3

Create Your Vision of Financial Wellness

I have learned this at least by my experiment: That if one advances confidently in the direction of his dreams, and endeavors to live the life which he has imagined, he will meet with a success unexpected in common hours.

—Henry David Thoreau

College students have a tendency to ask the question "why" a lot, and it seemed a particularly common question in Dr. Blancero's class. Back when I was working as a graduate assistant, a student asked why it was so important to write down goals. Always prepared, Dr. Blancero cited the results of an incredible research study.

In 1953, 3 percent of the students graduating from Harvard University that year actually wrote down their specific career goals. Twenty years later, in 1973, a study of that class showed that the 3 percent who had written down their career goals had accumulated more wealth than the other 97 percent—combined!

I had this thought in mind as I was waiting for Cindy and Scott at my "office" at Java Road. Most students assume that I'll start by talking about financial jargon like stocks and interest rates, but in this session, numbers are the last thing on my mind. Michelle had mentioned their credit card problems, but working that out would come later. My challenge in this session was to convince Cindy and Scott that despite their current financial troubles, they needed to do what those select Harvard students did in 1953: write down what they wanted to accomplish.

I had a feeling that Cindy and Scott wouldn't be as friendly as the first time I met them. After all, filling out the Vital Signs is not a fun exercise. Most people come to me looking for answers and tend to get frustrated when I give them mostly questions in return. Assessing oneself is never a comfortable exercise, but in order to improve in any area of life, you must first find out where you stand. We all have the building blocks to be successful; it's just a matter of piecing those blocks together. A self-assessment is the first step of any building process, and my first step in coming up with a prescription.

"Hi, Dr. Dink," Cindy said as she and Scott sat down with me at my usual booth. "Your speech was great and all, but let me warn you right now that I'm not in the best mood. I was up well past midnight preparing for a presentation I had to give at work. Plus, I had bill collectors hounding me all day, and to top it all off, there was some stockbroker in the office telling me that it's going to cost fifty bazillion dollars for college by the time my kids turn eighteen."

"Don't worry, Cindy, you and Scott are no different from most of my students," I said. "Let me first start with some parameters. Financial therapy is an active process—I do not give tips or hand out miracle drugs. You have to learn how to take care of your financial health and do your exercises. I only prescribe the medicine."

Cindy and Scott appeared to relax a little as I continued, "You can't beat yourself up when you don't see immediate results, and you must commit to doing your exercises. Once we are finished, you must commit to spending a half hour every month on your financial health."

"Already you sound like the rest of those financial gurus," said Cindy. "Let me guess—you're going to start by asking us to write down everything that we spent since kindergarten. Then you're going to tell us that we have too much credit card debt and that we're 'underinsured and underinvested.' Then you're going to sell us some miracle financial tool that lowers our monthly payments, provides peace of mind for our family, and will make us rich. We've heard the routine too many times. We don't want to feel like we are listening to another one of those infomercials."

"So why did you want to meet me in the first place?" I asked, and tried to read Cindy and Scott's body language. People are often leery of me at first—and it's not just because I walk around town wearing a white lab coat. In today's society, who actually dispenses advice without charging an arm and a leg? And when it comes to managing money, most professionals ask for a fee up front or take a percentage of the investors' assets, which often winds up costing thousands.

Scott spoke for the first time: "We thought you'd be different because you call yourself a doctor and we're really sick. That's why we're here. Truthfully, I think it's just a gimmick, but I figured we had nothing to lose. Plus, Michelle spoke pretty highly of you."

"What do you mean by *sick*?" I asked, ignoring the gimmick remark.

"Not only can we barely pay our bills," Cindy said, "but we can't get any new credit cards. We used to get three or four cards a week in the mail, and now we can't even use the ones that we have. Plus, that guy at work who was talking about the cost of college really got me scared."

This kind of response was typical and it reminded me of the first rule of holes, which states—if you are in one, stop digging. In a perfect world, people would come to see me before they got sick, but just as in the world of medicine, most wait until they're in bad shape to visit the Finance Doctor. Preventive medicine is hardly ever an option, but it was important to let Cindy and Scott know that it wasn't too late. "Let me see if the good doctor can put you at ease," I said. "First of all, I don't sell any products. The only service I offer is financial therapy, and it's free for friends and family. Think of me as your general practitioner. I will perform a diagnosis and provide you with a prescription to get well."

"Yeah, yeah," said Cindy. "You sound just like everyone else. You suck us in with the plan, or diagnosis, as you call it, and then *boom,* you sell us something or refer us to your cousin's girlfriend's sister's uncle who is giving you a kickback. We know the drill."

Although she was a bit more aggressive and more cynical than most students, I wasn't surprised by Cindy's continued skepticism and I countered it by being firm. "Cindy, I am not sucking you in with the diagnosis. The prescription is free, but you may find throughout the course of therapy that you need to buy some other products or services."

"Here it comes: Dr. Dink makes his move for our wallet," Scott said, jumping on the cynical bandwagon.

"Wrong again guys," I said emphatically. "In fact, an entire session is devoted to teaching you how to make major purchases. If I try to sell you something—and trust me, I won't—I wouldn't even let you buy it unless you shopped around."

Cindy still seemed uptight, and she said, "We're also concerned that we'll have to keep a log for every penny we spend. That's when all those financial gurus lose us, and we're flat out not doing it."

I had learned from experience that this was what turned people off the most. The best plan in the world isn't going to be effective unless it can be carried out. And at the end of the day, who really enjoys managing their finances? I know I don't. I would never take the time to write down every expense I incurred—not when there are baskets to shoot and guitars to strum. But the ramifications of not devoting a little bit of time to finances are so severe that most students don't mind spending that time, especially if they are working toward a goal.

I tried to impress all this upon Cindy and Scott when I said, "I don't blame you for not wanting to write down every expense, since I would never do so myself. In financial therapy, we try not to spend too much time going backward. We could spend years examining how you got sick and psychoanalyze why you overspend, but it wouldn't help you solve your current problems."

"Right on, Doc," Cindy said. "Too many of these finance gurus sound like my dad, a preacher, or a shrink."

"Can you read what that plaque on the wall says?" I asked as I pointed to the plaque that the owner of Java Road so graciously let me put on the wall.

"Sure," Cindy answered. "It says, 'Don't Preach—Teach.' And since you brought it up, I have a saying of my own, Doc: 'Don't Teach—Show.' There's no way we're going to meet you for an hour every week just to hear you talk."

That was music to my ears, and I replied, "Don't worry, most of your sessions will include field trips, and you will have the chance to talk with individuals who are experts in their professions."

"Field trips? Sounds exciting," said Scott. "And once we are finished with your financial therapy, we'll never have to think about our finances again?"

I thought back to Barry and Francis and how I taught them some quick tips on how to improve their SAT scores. I didn't want my new students falling into the same trap as those two. "Not so fast," I said. "Maintaining good financial health is a daily activity and you'll have to monitor your progress, but it shouldn't take more than a half an hour a month. Is that reasonable?"

"Sure, and then how often do we have to come back for check-ups?" asked Cindy.

"Ideally, you will never have to see me again. My objective is to teach you how to make good decisions so that you are not dependent on me. If you had to keep coming back, I would feel as if I had failed as a teacher. Just so we are clear, let me describe exactly what I do. *I teach financial therapy so that you can stop chasing your bills and start chasing your dreams.*"

They both nodded, and I continued, "I do not tell you how to get rich quick. I am not an investment guru or a stock market expert. I do not expect you to save your milk and cookies money and tear up all your credit cards. I simply want to teach you how to make smart decisions. You already heard me explain Q-Q-Kachoo in detail. That's the first step of an 8-step process. There are still seven more steps to go."

Somehow, I had struck a chord with Cindy. Sounding irritated, she said, "Why does money always have to be the central part of life? Happiness is not just about dollars and cents."

"Who said anything about money!" I exclaimed. In a stern voice, I said, "Let me repeat—*I teach financial therapy so that you can stop chasing your bills and start chasing your dreams.* When I ask people what really makes them tick, money rarely even makes the list."

"What does make the list?" asked Cindy, sounding skeptical.

"Here it is, short and sweet," I said as I handed Cindy and Scott an old prescription card with some notes written on it.

The Finance Doctor

℞

PEOPLE—Relationships with family, friends, and the community

HEALTH—How you feel physically

CAREER—Challenging, fulfilling day-to-day activities that are rewarding

Dr. Dink, MBA

After gazing down at the list, Cindy came at me again. "Doc, if money isn't important to you, then why do you teach people financial wellness for a living?"

I had heard this question many times before, and I gave her my standard response: "Because like it or not, money has the ability to impact all three of those things on that list. Marriages end and relationships go sour because of money. Professionally, most people use the excuse of money for not being passionate about their job. As for health, if you live in a place like Chicago, it's difficult to stay in shape in the winter if you can't afford to join a gym or buy a treadmill."

"What are you passionate about, Doc?" asked Scott.

"I am passionate about teaching people how to make good decisions and seeing the impact those decisions make on their lives. Getting their finances in order is simply a necessary evil along the way."

"So who do you consider a successful student?" asked Scott.

I loved all the questions. I think it's critical for my students to know where I come from, and I am happy to explain. I knew that by sharing my own career vision, it would ultimately help with today's exercises. I answered, "A successful student is one who meets the goals that they have outlined for themselves. Whether it's building their dream house or just paying off some of their debt, I work with students to help make their dreams a reality."

"Just so we know there is hope for us, can you give us an example?" asked Cindy.

Hope. It's what everyone always wants. It's why we buy lottery tickets and invest in penny stocks. The problem is that we look for hope from things that we have little control over. I knew it would be a challenge, but I had to teach Cindy and Scott that generating hope begins with creating a vision. Psychologists refer to it as the *power of visualization.*

Professional sports teams often pay sports psychologists hundreds of thousands of dollars to help athletes visualize, and there is little doubt that it's effective. When tennis star Venus Williams was interviewed after winning Wimbledon 2000, she said that she used to lie in bed at night and dream about winning the tournament. She believes in visualization so much that she went so far as to buy her gown for the Winner's Ball at Wimbledon—before the tournament even started!

Many golfers envision their stance, their swing, the impact of the club on the ball, the trajectory of the ball's flight, where the ball lands, and eventually, the ball rolling into the hole—before they even take a practice swing. Actresses are taught to envision the perfect performance before a show so that when it happens, it doesn't feel like the first time. Even my friend Roy, who is in sales, tells me that he actually visualizes his prospect signing a contract before he gives his sales pitch. If you picture yourself attaining a goal, chances are that you're going to get there.

To answer Cindy's question, I decided to use the obvious example to prove that my teaching could help. "Do you want an example?" I asked. "You already know Michelle. She earned her degree, is raising two beautiful kids, and is working in her dream job as an interior designer in her dream city of Boston."

"We know that already, which is why we agreed to see you in the first place," Cindy said. "What we want to know is how she did it. It just seems like such an uphill battle."

I knew exactly what Cindy and Scott really wanted to hear. They wanted to hear about a guy who had $50,000 worth of debt, bought a high-flying Internet stock that went through the roof, waxed his back, and retired to Tahiti. Like it or not, they were going to have to settle for the truth, so I replied, "The only way to reach your goals is to start figuring out what your goals actually are. If you don't have a map, you're going to end up lost."

When I worked for Dr. Blancero at ASU, the first assignment for our students was to read Stephen Covey's *The 7 Habits of Highly Effective People.* The book is about developing as a person, and it stresses the concept "Begin with End in Mind." Whether it's in the arts, sports, business, personal finance, or life, having a game plan is the first and most critical step.

From my research, I learned that a lot of people get intimidated when they hear the words "personal mission statement." But I also learned that people have no problem filling out a simple form. It's the blank page that they can't handle. Whether Cindy and Scott knew it or not, they had taken the first step toward creating a vision of financial wellness by filling out their diagnosis. When they went to get more coffee, I had a chance to look over their exercises from the previous week.

The Diagnosis

If we had more money, we would spend it on . . .
Travel, clothes, shoes, our kids, savings for education.

If we didn't have to work, we would spend our time . . .
Definitely not at our present jobs. We'd travel, shop, take classes, and spend more time with the kids.

Where does it hurt now?
Can't travel.
Bill collectors are hounding us.
Want to own a home but can barely pay the rent.
Stress—we're worried about our future.
No plan to pay for our kids' education.
We feel powerless over our finances.

What would make you feel better?
Winning the lottery.
A trip to the Greek islands.
Being able to pay our bills.
Feeling organized.
No more bill collectors.
Owning a house.
A savings plan for retirement and for our kids' education.

Are you taking any financial medicine?
We invest through our 401(k) plans at work.
We make the minimum payments on time for most of our bills.
We try to get as much credit as we can.

At the end of financial therapy, we hope to . . .
Have a plan to get out of debt.
Have a plan to own a home.
Understand investing and not be so intimidated.
Learn how to make a decision on going back to school.

When Cindy and Scott returned, I said out loud what I had been thinking. "After checking out the first part of your exercise, I am very pleased. You seem to have a good idea where you want to be."

"You obviously haven't seen the second part," said Cindy, referring to the Vital Signs.

When I had given Cindy and Scott their first exercises, I purposely didn't give them much direction on how to fill out their Vital Signs. I explained, "Your Vital Signs are simply what goes in and what goes out each month. I call them Vital Signs because they are the most important element of your financial health. No matter how much money you make or how you invest, you're never going to get very far if you're spending more than you make every month."

Cindy was already a step ahead of me: "But part of the reason we spend more than we make every month is all of the interest we pay on credit cards. When are we going to address that?" asked Cindy.

"Be patient," I said. "At this point, all I want you to do is see where you stand. I want to stress that *spending less than you make every month is the safest way to create wealth.*"

"I can handle that, Doc, but why did you make us do this first?" asked Cindy. "You promised that we wouldn't have to write down everything we spend."

I knew Cindy was stalling, which meant that their Vital Signs had to look pretty bad. Every student I meet thinks he or she is in the worst financial shape in the world, but most don't realize that spending more than you make has become the American way. I know it sounds ridiculous, but it's true. Think about the word "deficit." You probably first heard it in regards to the U.S. government. How can Uncle Sam expect us ordinary citizens to balance our budget when the country cannot even balance its own budget?

Rather than complain about our politicians, I tried a different approach with Cindy and Scott: "Think about how managing your finances is like losing weight. The Vital Signs are just like the scale. It's painful at first to step on and see how much you weigh. But once you do, you know where you stand and can begin to measure your progress. And after a few months, many of my students actually look forward to seeing their Vital Signs."

"This is going to be painful, Doc, so we might as well get it over with," said Scott as he handed me their Vital Signs.

I had designed the Vital Signs form with subtotals for each section, but I purposely left off a "Total" column on the bottom. You would think that most people would add it up anyway, but like Cindy and Scott, most do not for one simple reason—they are afraid to see how bad it really is. Michelle took over a year and a half before she would write down her monthly Vital Signs. Cindy and Scott were ahead of the game in that regard, and their willingness to do the exercises told me that they were at least "coachable."

Working quickly to add up the numbers, I didn't waste any time with the bad news and said, "You have $3,000 coming in and $4,220 going out, which means that you are running a monthly deficit of $1,220. Over the course of a year, you are making $36,000 and spending $50,640, for an annual deficit of $14,640. Keep in mind that your expenses do not include items such as vacations, emergencies, or gifts."

"You might as well add another grand for Christmas presents," Scott said, sounding defeated, "and I know there are some other things we forgot."

I filled in the three lines—and added a fourth line—of their Vital Signs myself and showed them to Cindy and Scott:

TOTAL MONTHLY INFLOWS	$3,000
TOTAL MONTHLY OUTFLOWS	$4,220
MONTHLY (DEFICIT)	**($1,220)**
ANNUAL (DEFICIT)	**($14,640)**

Monthly Vital Signs	
What's Coming In	
Take-home pay from primary jobs	3,000
Other income	0
TOTAL INFLOWS	**$3,000**
What's Going Out—Before We Get Out of Bed	
Rent/mortgage	900
Basic utilities—electricity, gas, water, basic phone	135
Renter's/homeowner's insurance	15
Car insurance—car 1	100
Car insurance—car 2	80
Life insurance (do not add if already taken out of take-home pay)	25
Additional medical insurance, including dental	25
Car payments—minivan	325
Car payments—convertible	275
Other monthly payments	0
Credit card payments	290
Student loans	150
TOTAL WHAT'S GOING OUT—BEFORE WE GET OUT OF BED	**$2,320**
What's Going Out—Basic Necessities	
Groceries—in-home eating	520
Basic clothing	150
Gas and car maintenance	200
Child care	280
Other—dry cleaning, laundry, cleaning supplies, etc.	50
Pet-related expenses	50
TOTAL WHAT'S GOING OUT—BASIC NECESSITIES	**$1,250**
What's Going Out—If You Had to Live Without	
Long-distance phone	120
Cable, basic and additional movie channels	50
Clothes and other shopping goodies	180
Toys, videos, music	80
Eating out	100
Cell phones	120
Household services—cleaning, lawn care	0
TOTAL WHAT'S GOING OUT—IF YOU HAD TO LIVE WITHOUT	**$650**

I knew Cindy and Scott were feeling down, but I wanted to make sure the impact of this deficit really hit home with them. I decided to go right for the jugular and matter-of-factly said, "So we can safely say that your daily lifestyle alone will mean that you will add over $15,000 to your debt in one year."

"I know this looks bad, but we are trying, Doc," said Cindy. "I heard this expert on TV say that you can save a lot of money by buying plane tickets twenty-one days in advance. I've also started waiting for sales at my favorite department stores. And Scott even talked to his boss about picking up some weekend shifts. It just seems like whatever we do, we can't win. And when I get frustrated, I have this bad habit of taking out my frustration at the shopping mall."

I had heard this kind of despair before, and I knew it was time to shift gears and display a kind bedside manner, so I said, "By preparing your Vital Signs, you *are* on the right track. The biggest challenge with most students is getting them to write down their goals and their Vital Signs. Once they do, they are almost certain to succeed in financial therapy. By the time we look at your Vital Signs again, you will be amazed at how much improvement you've made."

"That sounds kind of like a pep talk, Doc," said Scott. "You probably aren't used to meeting with people who are so financially irresponsible."

"That's what everybody thinks," I said. "But from my experience, whether my students are making $15,000, $50,000, or $150,000 a year, very few are able to make more than they spend. There are *sixty million* Americans with an average of $7,000 worth of credit card debt."

"For a change, I wish we were average," joked Cindy.

"At least it's good to see you smiling again, Cindy," I said. Now that we had gotten through most of the dirty work, it was time to actually create the vision for financial wellness. I had a simple questionnaire that made the process simple. And for this exercise, I felt it was critical to be there for my students.

Creating the Vision

Creating a vision of financial wellness is not complicated. It's just that in the scheme of life, we often forget to take the time to figure out what it is we really want. And because money is often the answer in the short run, it's easy to lose sight of what really makes us tick. I myself fell prey to this when I got away from my dream of being a teacher by overspending and getting trapped in a job that I did not enjoy.

Creating a vision starts by identifying what financial wellness looks like. For some it's material wealth, and for others it's peace of mind. I tell my students to focus on how financial wellness will make them feel. The second step is to write down goals that meet these four criteria. Goals must be *specific*, *challenging*, *attainable*, and *have a deadline*. It's important to think big and not leave off goals that may seem to be a bit of a reach. Then list your dreams—and don't worry, you can shoot for the stars. Dreams remind you of why you are working so hard and that anything is possible.

After explaining all this to Cindy and Scott, I wanted them to concentrate on thinking, not writing, so I scribbled as they spoke. When we finished, their vision looked like this.

Cindy and Scott's Vision of Financial Wellness

Financial Wellness Is . . .

Not always feeling so stressed about money
Working in a job that we love
Not being afraid or depressed every time we get a bill in the mail
Owning a home
Feeling comfortable about how much we are saving for education
Investing wisely
Having enough savings to take care of our kids now and our parents later

Goals . . .

Start a college fund for the kids—deadline: 3 months
Pay off all our credit card debt—deadline: 1 year
Travel overseas—deadline: 2 years
Own a home—deadline: 3 years

Dreams . . .

Retire before the age of fifty
Send our kids to college without having to take out loans
Own a beach house
Travel to six continents
Have only one of us working at a time
Drive a '57 Chevy and a pink Cadillac

When I finished writing, I handed the piece of paper to Cindy and Scott, who seemed unimpressed. "This is it?" exclaimed Cindy. "Creating your vision is nothing more than a piece of scrap paper?"

I explained to Cindy that by writing down her vision, we accomplish three things. The first is that we establish our objective for going through financial therapy. When students get frustrated, I often go back to the vision and remind them of why they came to see me in the first place. The second is that it creates attainable goals that can be measured. And last, it reminds them that in order to fulfill a dream, they must start by having a dream. To dream the impossible is the first step in making it possible.

I wasn't quite finished and explained that they now had two tasks to perform with their vision. The first was to make it visual by creating symbols that remind them of their goals. My friend Bobby has a picture of his dream home on the mirror in his bathroom to remind him of his goal of owning a home. My Aunt Pinkie wrote down her goals on a piece of paper and had it laminated. She keeps it in her purse so she can constantly refer to it. My friend George keeps a picture of a Ferrari in his wallet to remind him of his dream car.

The second assignment was to share their vision with the people in their life who could help them achieve it. To accentuate this point, I decided to tell them the story of the Three Dreaming Crabs. I started, "Back in Maryland, where I grew up, there were three crabs, Dale, David, and Darren, and each of them lived in a bucket. The first crab, Dale, lived in a bucket with a group of negative, mean-spirited crabs. Every time he tried to crawl out of the bucket to fulfill his dream of making it to the beach, one of the other crabs would reach up with one of his claws and drag Dale back down to the bottom. It was a sad existence for Dale, and because of the company he kept, he was never able to fulfill his dream."

"What about the other two?" asked Scott.

"The second crab, David, lived in a bucket all by himself. Every time he tried to crawl out to fulfill his dream of making it to the beach, it was a constant struggle, but since there were no other crabs pulling him down, he sometimes made it. His problem was that when he reached the beach, there was no one there to share the joy with him, which ultimately left him feeling unfulfilled. Even worse, the times that he fell to the bottom of the bucket, there was no one there to pick him back up."

"And what about the third crab?" asked Cindy.

"The third crab, Darren, lived in a bucket with other positive, dreaming crabs with whom he felt comfortable sharing his vision. Funny, they all shared the same dream of climbing out of the bucket and making it to the beach. Whenever Darren would try to crawl out of the bucket, the other crabs would lend a claw and give him a boost. All of the crabs worked together, and ultimately, they were all able to accomplish their dream of getting out of the bucket and making it to the beach. Once they got there, they felt an enormous sense of love and satisfaction from being around others who had shared in their vision."

"Wow, that's some story," said Cindy. "Sometimes I get the feeling that I live in the same bucket as Dale. It seems like there are so many people who are quick to point out the negatives and discourage us from following our heart."

I knew what Cindy meant. Only after years of really finding out who my true friends were was I able to find the perfect mix of people with whom I felt comfortable sharing my dreams. And once I did, my life started to look a lot more like the life of Darren the crab.

Think about who embraces your dreams and share your vision with those people. And just as important, be sure to stay away from the cancerous crabs in your life who only want to pull you down and prevent you from chasing your dreams.

Preparing for Next Week

The order of my prescription is no accident. The first thing I like to address is the importance of decision making. By introducing Q-Q-Kachoo and walking through the three steps, it lets students learn what financial therapy is all about. Once the student decides to move forward, it's time to gather information and begin to formulate a prescription. Then I can explain financial therapy and help the students create their vision of financial wellness.

I said to Cindy and Scott, "Next session, we are going to talk about making big purchases. For your exercises, you need to get three price quotes on all types of insurance. That includes life insurance, medical insurance, renter's insurance, and insurance for both of your cars."

"Why all the trouble?" asked Scott.

"My friend Dr. Howard just moved to Los Angeles and wanted to buy a BMW convertible. He's a pediatrician and has very little time to shop around, which is why he usually just buys from the first place he goes. But when it came time to buy the convertible, he got four bids: two in person and two over the Internet."

"Sounds like a lot of time for a pediatrician to spend shopping for a car," said Cindy.

"I don't think Dr. Howard would agree with you. The cheapest bid was $39,400 and the most expensive bid was for $44,200, which is a difference of $4,800. Even for a doctor, $4,800 is a lot of money for only two hours of work."

"What kind of idiot would pay almost five thousand bucks more for the same exact car that another dealer is selling?" asked Scott.

"Somebody is keeping that dealership in business," I said, "and I know Dr. Howard is happy it's not him." I thought back to all the people who had bought windows from me without shopping around. *They* were the "idiots" who were keeping that dealership in business. Perhaps I should be more politically correct and use the word *uneducated consumers* instead of idiots. But if I offend those who don't do their homework before making big purchases, all the better. Dr. Howard was so offended that he went out and saved close to five thousand bucks.

Cindy saved herself from hearing one of my lectures when she said, "Don't worry, we'll get the insurance quotes."

After Cindy and Scott left, I looked over their Vital Signs and took a deep breath. It wasn't as if I hadn't seen worse, but I was still a little concerned. I knew that paying close attention to all the stages of financial therapy was the only solution. In my line of work, there are no shortcuts.

Exercise 3

A. Create your vision of financial wellness
Financial Wellness is . . .

Goals . . .

Dreams . . .

B. Create visuals so that you can "see" your vision every day.

C. Share your vision with the right "Dreaming Crabs."

D. Get three quotes on all types of insurance:

	Company 1	Company 2	Company 3
Car 1			
Car 2			
Life			
Medical			
Homeowner's/Renter's			
Other			

Chapter 4

Use the Buyer's Antibiotic For Big Purchases

It is preoccupation with possessions, more than anything else, that prevents us from living freely and nobly.

—Bertrand Russell

Preparing for this session always brings back memories of growing up, especially since my parents always found a way to get a good deal on just about everything they bought. It didn't matter if it was my dad's new DustBuster or my mom's new blender, my parents always found the lowest possible price.

Before my brother went to college, he was selected to play in the "Big 33," a high school football all-star game in Hershey, Pennsylvania, that pitted the thirty-three best high school football players from Maryland against the thirty-three best from Pennsylvania. When my dad got the news, he knew that it was not only going to be an incredible event, but an expensive one as well.

Part of his job as an accountant was to plan company meetings and negotiate with hotels, so he knew all the tricks to getting the best deal. But for this game, which brought more than 20,000 people to town, the hotels in Hershey jacked up their prices. The term for this is gouging, a common practice in the travel industry, and one for which there is no remedy—for most people. After being quoted an absurd rate for the weekend, my dad called back a day later, disguised his voice, and said he was a coach for the Maryland team. Within seconds, his rate was cut in half.

My brother and I somehow found out about my dad's little trick and could not stop teasing him about it, especially since he was always preaching to us about ethics. He tried to rationalize it by saying that he was simply playing by the rules of the hotel business, in which just about every customer pays a different price—depending on how well they negotiate. What my brother and I knew was that the man who had lectured us on ethics for countless hours had pulled a scheme himself. For two years, whenever the subject of ethics came up, Andy and I would refer to our dad as "Coach."

It eventually got to him, and two years later, when I was selected to play in the Big 33, my dad did not take the hotel decision lightly. Instead, he did a Q-Q-Kachoo, and the components looked something like this:

Quantitative—The Numbers:
"I'll save $300 by saying I'm a coach."

Qualitative—Ben Franklin:

Pros	**Cons**
The hotel is the most convenient place to stay.	It is unethical.
No one will get hurt, and I'm saving money.	I am *really* tired of being called Coach.

Kachoo:
"It feels wrong. It was wrong of the hotel to price gouge because of the game, but it was just as wrong for me to lie the last time. I

couldn't even look the other parents in the eye, knowing that they were paying twice as much. It also makes me sick to give a hotel my business when they are being so unethical."

After doing his Q-Q-Kachoo, my dad decided to trade convenience for peace of mind and booked a hotel a half hour away from where the game was being held. From this experience, I learned two key things that I could pass on to my students. The first is that just about everything in life is negotiable, and those who ask for a better price often get it. I also learned that making a good purchase is not only measured by money. There is no better way to waste money than to buy something that you can't use or that ultimately makes you feel lousy.

It's real-life stories, such as the one about my dad, that my students can relate to best. My students also tell me that they appreciate getting information "straight from the horse's mouth," which is why I try so hard to arrange for experts to meet with my students. Thankfully, my brother, Andy, was in town, and I knew that after ten years of working in sales, he would provide a fresh perspective for Cindy and Scott.

"Have a seat, guys," I said from my familiar booth at Java Road when Cindy and Scott came in for the next session. "Just so you know, I talk about how to make big purchases early in therapy because, after preparing their Vital Signs, many of my students start clipping coupons and taking a lot of small steps to help them on the road to financial well-being."

"So I can throw away the coupons from Sunday's newspaper?" asked Scott.

"Not just yet, but here is a good rule of thumb," I said as I scribbled on a prescription card:

The Finance Doctor

℞

The bigger the purchase, the more time you should spend getting competitive prices.

Dr. Dink, MBA

"Wow! That's earth-shattering, Doc," Cindy said sarcastically. "Did you think of that nugget of wisdom all by yourself?"

"I know it sounds too basic to even bother stating, but it is critical," I said. "My friend Abigail will spend hours clipping coupons to save a few bucks, but then will turn around and spend thousands of dollars on insurance after meeting with only one insurance company. It's typical behavior and it's why I devote an entire session to large purchases. Speaking of which, what did you learn from getting three bids on all types of major insurance?"

"We learned that there are dozens of companies selling the same thing for dozens of prices," Scott said, and he was right. "I thought stuff like insurance was regulated and that the price was set by the government or something and so you just picked a company because the agent was nice."

"You're not alone in your thinking," I said. A lot of my students think the same exact thing until they actually take the time to get three bids. And in the few instances that the prices aren't all that different, they at least walk away with the satisfaction of knowing that they didn't get ripped off. When you get three bids, you assure that you will never be the sucker. With auto insurance, there is almost always a significant savings, and I was anxious to see what they came up with. Cindy had her notebook out.

"The car insurance on my convertible is $1,200 per year, and it's $960 on our minivan," said Cindy. "Scott and I use a different company because we've each been with our insurance companies for so long and they always told us that it's cheaper if you stay with the same company. But when we started getting quotes, we were told that you can get a discount if you have more than one car. So we had all three companies give us prices based on two cars. Here are the quotes."

Car	Current Premium	Company X	Company Y	Company Z
Convertible	$1,200	$1,250	$925	$950
Minivan	$960	$950	$700	$735
Total	$2,160	$2,200	$1,625	$1,680

"Keep in mind," I said, "that you don't always buy based on price, especially for insurance. What's the point of buying insurance if the company isn't going to be around to help you with your questions and needs?"

"I agree, Doc," said Scott, "which is why I researched companies X, Y, and Z, and I wasn't comfortable with the fast-talking agent from Y. But Z is the current company that Cindy uses, and they have been great to her over the years. Plus, to insure the minivan, they are going to charge $735 instead of the $960 that we're already paying for the exact same coverage. So how much are we saving overall?"

"Forty bucks a month, which comes out to $480 a year. And all it cost you was half an hour," I said, sounding very much like one of those insurance commercials. "Before you meet my brother,

Andy, I want to give you his list of rules for making big purchases. He should be here any minute."

Andy's Rules for Making Big Purchases

1. Getting a "good deal" isn't a reason to buy something.
2. Make a list of exactly what you want before you go shopping.
3. Decide on your ideal price as well as a maximum price before you go shopping.
4. Get a minimum of three bids on purchases over $100.
5. Make sure you are comparing apples to apples—*not* apples to oranges.
6. Add it up to the reality.
7. Understand the cost to buy versus the cost to own.
8. Go to an "independent source" like *Consumer Reports* to get objective advice.
9. Learn to "debunk the myth."
10. Apply Q-Q-Kachoo and be sure to double-check your gut.

As Cindy and Scott studied the list, my brother came into the room with his usual energy. "Dr. Dink, I see you have a few more students in need of big brother's wisdom."

Andy was the perfect person to teach this part of therapy. For one, he is an incredible salesperson—and I'm not just saying that because he's my big brother. At the age of twenty-nine, the *Charlotte Business Journal* recognized him as one of the Top 40 Business Leaders Under 40 in the city of Charlotte, North Carolina. The only thing that bugs me about Andy is that despite being two years older than I, he has a full head of hair, while I've been using Rogaine ever since I was twenty-four—with some success, I might add.

Andy needed to pick up a Buyer's Antibiotic form—something that Cindy and Scott were soon to be very familiar with—that he had left with a kitchen remodeling company. We decided to kill two birds with one stone and teach this session in the car on the way to the company's office. I figured that it would be best if we all went for a ride in Andy's convertible—mainly so I could experience the sensation of the wind blowing through my hair, while I still had it. Andy and I had already planned to go through his list, top to bottom, and let Cindy and Scott ask questions along the way.

We all jumped into the convertible, and as soon as he heard the click of the seat belts, Andy fired away in the southern drawl he had picked up after living in North Carolina for twelve years. "Back when I was buying furniture for my house, my little bro started lecturing me about how to make big purchases. Now I've been in sales for almost ten years, and there wasn't a darn thing I could learn from him about buying."

Andy was right that knowledge was not his problem. His problem was actually putting that knowledge to use when he was a buyer and not the seller. What made him such a good salesman was his ability to create emotion, but when he was on the other side, he often got swept up in the emotion himself and bought on impulse. He argued that his time was valuable and he couldn't be bothered with shopping around. He cut me off when I tried to tell him about my friend Dr. Howard, the guy who saved almost $5,000 by shopping around for his car.

"My problem wasn't knowing *how* to be a good buyer," my brother said, "it was actually being one. Let's start with rule number one. Getting a 'good deal' isn't a reason to buy something. Our aunt Beezie used to buy dozens of corn dogs when they were on sale simply because they were on sale. Every time we went over there, we'd have to sneak our uneaten lunches out to the trash so we wouldn't hurt her feelings. I learned that buying something you don't need *at any price* drains your wallet and usually just clutters your closet or your refrigerator."

Andy had made a good point, and he certainly had Cindy and Scott's attention. He continued, "Next is deciding on your own criteria. Pretend you are buying a car. The salesperson might try to sell you on the importance of wood paneling or a CD player, even though those items are not important to you."

"Like when the TV salesman kept insisting that we get Surround Sound when all we wanted was the big screen," said Scott.

"Exactly," said Andy. "That's why *you* make a list to make sure *you* get what's important, not the salesman," said Andy. "You also want to set a price in your mind so you can set a limit for yourself by establishing a maximum value you are willing to pay for something. I can tell you from experience that a salesperson has a million reasons to convince you to spend more than you want. Whatever they're selling is the most important thing in the world to them, and they try to convince you that you shouldn't let money stop you from getting the best."

"They always tell me that I deserve it," Scott said. "They tell me that by buying the better product, I am being good to myself—and if I don't, I'm cheating myself."

As the little brother, I had to know when to pick my spots to chime in, and now was as good a time as any, so I said, "Salesmen need to sell to make a living. I used to say the same things every day. Just remember, these guys are saying these things so they can accomplish *their* goals. Having a list and a price target will remind you of your own goals. Every salesperson will tell you that you're getting a good deal, but what is something really worth?"

"What the market says it's worth," answered Scott.

"You got it, and the market is nothing more than every buyer and seller in the world," said Andy, picking up just where I had left off. "I may not have an MBA like my little brother, but I know that the only way to find out if you're getting a good price is to shop around and see what prices are out there. Just because an item is reduced or on sale doesn't mean you are getting a good deal—because a lot of these stores mark up their prices on purpose just so they can pretend to have a sale."

Andy was on a roll now and didn't come up for air. "That's one of the tricks. But as a buyer, your tricks are *research* and *patience.* Rule four reminds you to get a minimum of three bids on purchases over $100. The Internet makes it easy to do the research, and even if you don't have a computer, the Yellow Pages or just old-fashioned window shopping can work just as well. Salespeople will typically use some sort of impending doom trick to get you to buy immediately. Sometimes they'll tell you that it's the last one or the deal is only good for one day."

"I've heard those lines before, but I still fall for them," Scott said. "They also remind me how valuable my time is and that I came to the store to get what I needed, not to get back in my car and shop for the rest of the day."

"That's a good point," said Andy, "and it's the reason that you don't have to go to five stores to buy pig's feet and vinegar. Remember that the more money you are going to spend, the more research you should do. For $12,000 worth of remodeling, do your homework. But it's not going to kill you if you pay a quarter too much for toilet paper. By the time you go to five stores, you just might—"

"Okay, let's keep this on a need-to-know basis only," interrupted Cindy thankfully. Details aside, I felt that Andy was really starting to reach them, but I wanted to jump back for a second and talk more about "impending doom," so I asked Scott, "Why do you think salespeople are so anxious for you to buy on the spot, aside from the fact that they want to get paid right away?"

"Maybe because they're afraid you'll find a better deal if you look around," Scott said right away.

He was dead-on, and Andy explained further: "You bet, and if they're afraid of that, you can be sure that there is a better deal elsewhere. Professional salespeople who sell products and services that offer the best value will actually encourage you to look around."

"I just feel so guilty when a salesperson is so nice and considerate, and then I don't buy from them," said Cindy.

I had heard this quite a few times before, and it frustrated me to no end. Why my students feel a sense of loyalty to a salesperson who is simply trying to get into their wallet is beyond me, but rather than get mad, I said to Cindy, "Then just tell the salesperson up front that you will get several bids. This way you don't have to feel guilty, since you were up front with them from the beginning. Plus, you will get much better service and a better price."

"I don't get it," said Scott, and I could see why. Most buyers just want to deal with someone honest, yet most salespeople insist on playing games. I let Andy explain.

"Because the only thing we salespeople hate more than not getting a sale is letting our competitors get a sale that we had a chance to bid on," said Andy. "So the minute the salesperson knows that you are looking at the competition, he or she will bend over backward to educate you and give you the best price."

"But that could lead to even more guilt," said Cindy.

"Cindy, when you go to buy something, is your goal to get the best value or to make the salesperson happy?" asked Andy, who had a way of making someone see his point.

"Point taken," said Cindy, "but I just can't stand all the pressure, and it's tough not to buy from the person who spent the most time with me."

"I agree," said Andy, "which is why I give the most considerate salespeople all they could ever ask for. I give them last look. It means that I will give a salesperson a chance to make another bid before I make a final decision, and it works for two reasons. The first is that you don't feel guilty because you can explain to the salesperson that the other product had better features or a better price. The second reason is that many salespeople will make a counteroffer and give you an even better deal."

"Why don't they give us the best price up front?" asked Scott, who was coming around slowly on this one. For those who aren't in sales, it's hard to believe that it's all one big game created to make money off naive consumers.

"We don't make the rules, we just got to live by 'em," I told Scott. "In a perfect world, salespeople would just give you their best price up front. But the way the system works, the customers who do the most homework pay the least."

"Just like Mom and Dad," said Andy as he looked at me. "Remember how we used to tease them for always shopping at Syms, that discount store? How many times did Dad repeat their motto, 'An Educated Consumer Is Our Best Customer'?"

"More than I care to remember," I answered. "But the funny thing is, the minute we had to start paying for our own clothes, we started shopping there, too, and haven't stopped yet."

Scott must have heard enough of our childhood stories. Either that, or he was thinking about how unpleasant salespeople had made his life over the years, because he interrupted our conversation and said, "I think I understand the game guys, but I don't like playing it. I have better things to do than listen to a bunch of salesmen's hullabaloo."

"Me too," said Andy, "which is why my brother and I developed the Buyer's Antibiotic. Whenever we go to make a major purchase, we hand the salesperson one simple sheet of paper."

Buyer's Antibiotic

I am in the market to purchase __________________. I will be obtaining several bids before making a decision. In order to consider your company for my purchase, I need the following information:

The *total price,* including any and all related costs, is:

The *total price* can be broken down as follows:

The biggest advantage of my product/service is:

The biggest disadvantage of my product/service is:

List three to five reasons why I should do business with you:

Please list five references, including phone numbers:

"Andy, you know as well as I do that they never give you the price without boring you with their long sales pitch," said Scott.

"It depends on the situation," my brother replied. "If you're getting bids on car insurance and know exactly the coverage you need, you should be able to get this information right off the bat. But if you're setting up a trust or a will, the price is going to depend on your specific needs. That's why rule five is to compare apples to apples, not apples to oranges."

That was just Andy's way of saying that you need to be sure you are comparing similar products. It's quite easy for appliances or computers, but it can be difficult for other items, especially services such as remodeling.

At that point, Andy pulled into a strip mall and told us he would be just a few minutes. When he came back, he showed us the Buyer's Antibiotic that he had just picked up from the kitchen store. Just as I had hoped, Andy was finally starting to listen to his little brother. The form looked like this:

Buyer's Antibiotic

I am in the market to purchase kitchen remodeling. I will be obtaining several bids before making a decision. In order to consider your company for my purchase, I need the following information:

The *total price,* including any and all related costs, is:
$12,000

The *total price* can be broken down as follows:

Appliances:	$6,000
Labor:	$5,000
Warranties:	$1,000

The biggest advantage of my product/service is:
Attention to detail, and well-trained staff who take pride in their work.

The biggest disadvantage of my product/service is:
We're not the cheapest guys in town and we're not the fastest.

List three to five reasons why I should do business with you:
We have been in business for thirty-five years.
We use the best-quality products.
Our technicians are professionally trained.
Our warranty is the best in the industry.

Please list five references, including phone numbers:

The Shulmans	555-5278
Lo-ee Blanken	555-1119
Phil & Shirley	555-4733
Jack & Jodi	555-5151
Ellie May	555-9464

I was impressed that my brother had finally taken the time to *use* the Buyer's Antibiotic instead of just talking about it. He once hired the cheapest painter in town without getting any references, thinking he could save a few bucks. Ultimately, he ended up with a bunch of headaches, a house that still needed to be painted, and a lawsuit.

Shifting the focus back to Andy's list, Scott said, "I don't understand rule six. What does it mean to 'add it up to the reality'?"

This was my favorite rule, so I picked up the ball and said, "When I started in sales, I was trained to 'break it down to the ridiculous.' In other words, if I was selling something for $100, I'd say, 'That's about eight bucks a month,' or, 'That's less than two bucks a week.' Sometimes I'd even say, 'That's only twenty-eight cents a day. I bet twenty-eight cents falls out of your pocket every day. You could probably pay for this thing with money you find in between the cushions in your couch.'"

"You were pretty slick," said Cindy.

"He's so slick that now he teaches his students that whenever a salesperson breaks it down to the ridiculous, they should *add it up to the reality*," said Andy. "Don't let a salesperson suck you in by breaking the overall price down into small payments. Always figure out the total purchase price before you buy anything. If they say thirty bucks a month, you think $360 a year. If they say twenty bucks a week, you think $1,040 a year."

"And be sure to look at the final purchase price, including interest," I added, practically shouting out this point as I was thinking back to my days selling home improvements. "You wouldn't believe this, but it's not uncommon for people to buy $5,000 worth of windows priced out over thirty years. At $84 a month, that adds up to over thirty grand!"

Andy quickly cut in, knowing that I was bound to go off on a tangent, and said, "That leads perfectly into rule seven: Don't just think about the cost to buy, think about the cost to own."

"Like for a car, you have to add in the cost of maintenance, repairs, insurance, gas, parking, and all that stuff," Scott said.

"Right. And sometimes the cost to buy for one product will be cheaper than another, but the upkeep is more expensive," said Andy. "You need to be especially careful of products, such as mobile phones, that are free. 'Free' products and services usually end up costing you the most. And those 'trial' memberships usually get you into a lot of trouble."

A good example of the cost to buy versus the cost to own is a boat. Buying one is expensive enough, but when you add the cost of maintenance, gas, insurance, and docking fees, you quickly realize why owning a boat is usually reserved for the very rich. Something else to think about is a new furnace or any other energy-saving device. The cost to buy is often expensive, but the cost to own—in this case, your monthly utility bills—can often mean that you save money. In other words, it costs more *not to buy* than to buy.

Cindy and Scott could hardly take in the information fast enough, and Andy kept rolling through the list: "Rule number eight is pretty straightforward—ask someone you know and respect who is an expert on the subject, or go to an independent source like *Consumer Reports* or *Consumers Digest* to get objective advice."

I thought this was an important point, so I added, "Be sure the person giving you advice doesn't have any motive, and if you are dealing with a salesperson, you can be pretty darn sure that they have a motive and they are not being objective. Talking to a friend who is in the business of what you are looking for is a good place to start. But even then, you have to be careful. Finding somebody objective often takes work."

"That makes sense," Scott said. "But what about number nine? I can't imagine what it means to 'debunk the myth.'"

"That's not on my list of rules," Andy said with a look of confusion on his face.

"That's because I just added it today," I said. "Last night, Darius introduced me to his friend Ian, who owns a chain of gas stations. Ian explained to me that he sells his gas for a lower price than his competitors, even though it's exactly the same product. He told me that the guy across the street, with a well-known brand-name gas station, not only sells the *exact same gas,* but also buys the gas from the *exact same distributor.*

"This guy Ian must not know anything about sales and marketing," Andy joked. The funny thing is, that was my first reaction when Ian told me the story. Then he explained that his biggest challenge was to "debunk the myth."

I tried to sum up Ian's explanation. "He told me that the reason the other guy can charge more is that his company has spent, and continues to spend, millions of dollars on marketing. When people like you and me are constantly exposed to their advertisements, we start to believe that their brand is better."

"But if Ian's product is the same, enough people will soon realize that, and eventually, he'll get all the business because of his cheaper prices," said Scott.

"You are absolutely right, Scott, and that's why as customers become more and more educated, Ian's business is growing. My dad always bought gas from the cheapest station, and my brother and I do, too. But let's leave Ian to figure out his own marketing strategy and talk about how debunking the myth affects you. In short, don't rely on advertisers to do your research for you."

Andy put it another way: "You don't have to read the labels on everything. In my business, gas is one of my biggest expenses, so it's worth it for me to do my research. I also eat out most of the time, so I don't need to worry if I pay a couple of cents too much when I buy dishwashing detergent. When it comes to products that I buy frequently, I take the time to do my homework. For example, if you spend a lot of money on prescription drugs, don't ask Dr. Dink if you should buy generics—ask your medical doctor. My doctor tells me that most generic drugs are exactly the same as the name brands, and that allows me to save a fortune. Marketing has become such a force in our society that half the time, we don't know what we are buying. Just be sure to listen to objective experts and not the marketers who make a living off of your naiveté."

It just didn't seem fair that Andy got the hair and the way with words, but as usual, he said it better than I did. The last rule—apply Q-Q-Kachoo and be sure to double-check your gut—I didn't have to explain. Big purchases and big decisions are often one and the same.

Cindy and Scott thanked Andy for the crash course as he dropped us back at Java Road. Scott must have really been moved by this session because he was in an incredible hurry to get to work. Before we even ordered our coffee, Scott took out his notes and said, "Let me show you what else we came up with from our exercises. The renter's insurance was all within a couple of bucks, so we're going to keep what we have."

"That's fine," I said. "But keep in mind, you can often get a discount if you use the same company for renter's insurance that you use for your car insurance."

"We thought of that, Doc," said Scott, "but they were still about the same price. The tough part was the medical and life. It was impossible to get quotes since we didn't know what to compare. Plus, neither of us was even sure how much insurance we needed, much less what we already have from work."

"There's a way to find out," I said.

"You are so predictable, Doc," said Scott, "which is why we beat you to the punch. Cindy and I checked our policies at work, and it turns out we don't need the extra medical insurance. Looking back on it, we got talked into that by some smooth insurance salesman. We have been throwing away $25 a month for three years."

Insurance is often a difficult topic to discuss since it is so hard to put a price tag on peace of mind. The insurance salesperson is always going to tell you that you don't have enough, but how do you really know? I'm the kind of person who doesn't like to buy warranties on appliances, but I stop short of giving that advice. When it comes to buying insurance, it is critical to think hard about the price you are willing to pay for peace of mind, because that is exactly what you are buying and there is not necessarily a wrong or a right answer—but there is a right approach, and it always starts with getting three bids.

Scott continued: "We really got confused about life insurance—

there's whole life, term, annuities. The whole thing is so confusing, and we don't know who the heck to trust."

I knew where Scott was coming from, and I had learned over the years that often, the best place to turn is to your employer. I said, "The first place I would go is to the benefits department of your company. Companies create Human Resources departments to help their employees with these types of questions, but so few ever take advantage of the knowledge. Like I told you the first day we started, I am a general practitioner and I don't have all the answers."

"And what if we decide to go directly to an insurance agent?" asked Scott, who apparently didn't want to heed my advice and check with his company.

"Just remember what Andy taught you. An agent's job is to sell life insurance, so they are going to be biased. But if you get at least three quotes, you are at least off on the right foot."

"Can you at least give us a place to start?" asked Cindy.

"I typically recommend term life insurance," I said. "Term life insurance is basic insurance—you pay a premium and your beneficiaries receive a set amount upon death. Other policies, such as whole or universal life, combine investing with insurance and sound good on the surface, but are poor investments. A good rule of thumb is to buy a term life insurance policy that equals six to eight times your annual salary. So, for you two, that would be between $150,000 and $200,000 each."

Cindy and Scott talked back and forth and realized that they each had over $200,000 worth of life insurance from their respective employers and also had sufficient health coverage. With this knowledge, we revised their insurance outflows.

Monthly Outflow	**Previous**	**Current**	**Difference**
Car insurance	$180	$140	$40
Extra life insurance	$25	$0	$25
Extra medical insurance	$25	$0	$25
Total Monthly Insurance Savings			**$90**

"Your car payment isn't going to change until you buy a new one," I said, "but at least you know how to be smarter about buying a car. Based on what you have told me, it sounds like the life and medical insurance you receive from work is sufficient. Be sure to verify this, but once you do, you can cancel those other policies."

Putting $90 back in the Vital Signs certainly made this lesson worthwhile. I also knew that the real savings would be in the future, when bigger purchases—such as a house, a mortgage, and a new car—would be made. By showing Cindy and Scott the perspective of a salesman like Andy, I knew the lessons would stick.

Preparing for Next Week

The next session was one of my favorites, since students really got to see how a little bit of work can lead to thousands of dollars in savings. Learning to beat the credit card companies and banks isn't too hard if you know how to play the game. I said to Scott and Cindy, "For next week, I need statements for all of your loans, including credit cards. I also need bank statements."

"Speaking of loans, my brother Brent is having problems in that area as well," said Cindy. "Would you mind if I brought him along next week?"

"You should already know the answer to that question," I said. "I cannot give financial therapy without a complete diagnosis."

"But he's got bill collectors all over him and he needs help paying off his credit cards," said Cindy.

"Does he own a home?" I asked, seeking an opportunity.

"For now!" teased Scott.

"For your benefit, I will make an exception and allow you to bring him along. One day, you two will be homeowners, and I'd like you to see how a home can make a huge impact on your financial health." I knew that the lesson on home equity loans was an important one.

"See you next week," said Cindy. "You got a real challenge on your hands with Brent."

"No I don't. Katie does."

"Sounds like another field trip," said Cindy. "Where are we going, and who's Katie?"

"It's up to Katie if you go anywhere, but I would be willing to bet that you will be headed to the mall," I said. "And, by the way, Katie's the vice president of a major bank in town and she's one tough cookie, so be prepared."

Exercise 4

Make a list of all your debt with an interest rate above 10 percent. Include the interest rates and the current balance. Look through your last three bank statements and bring them along.

Example

Creditor	Type	Interest Rate	Balance
Visa	Credit card	18%	$5,000
Department store	Credit card	21%	$2,500
Appliance store	Credit card	23%	$1,200

Creditor	Type	Interest Rate	Balance

Chapter 5

Enjoy the Money You Earn—Stop Giving It to the Banks

Money provides the luxury of making choices, but it does not bring happiness, contentment, or fulfillment. That is a state of mind that has to be about how you feel about yourself when you go to sleep.

—Andre Agassi

My friend Katie would argue that a good dose of materialism can be a great motivator. On her way up the corporate ladder, Katie embraced the concept "dress for success," and to accomplish her vision of becoming a vice president of a major national bank, she dedicated a huge chunk of her Vital Signs to her apparel. When we talked about her strategy one day at the pool of her oceanfront condominium, Katie told me how she did it, and the mistakes she made along the way.

For every material purchase Katie made, she viewed it as an investment. Whether it was her purse, her briefcase, shoes, or the kind of car she drove, she always created an image of success. Even back when she was making only $12,000 a year, she would wear only $100 blouses and wouldn't be caught dead without her Louis Vuitton purse. What people didn't see was the mess that her finances looked like behind the scenes. She quickly learned that much of her bank's revenue came from customers paying high interest and fees, and it dawned on her one day that the banks were getting rich off naive customers—and she was one of them!

After going to her employer for an installment loan and consolidating her debt to lower interest loans, she was able to erase almost $10,000 worth of credit debt in less than a year. She then got rid of all her department store and credit cards, and replaced them with just one American Express. Back then, AmEx required that bills get paid in full each month. The card was for convenience only—not credit—and it provided the wake-up call that Katie needed to stop buying things she couldn't afford.

Getting that AmEx card helped, but more important, making a commitment never to spend more than she makes every month has enabled her to thrive financially. She's a model student, and while some think that financial therapy is about sacrifices, I remind them that successful students are ones who have met the goals that they have outlined. I put Katie at the top of this list, and with a combination of a clear vision and sound decision making, she has reached the pinnacle in her field. Enjoying material things along the way has been a pleasure that she has earned.

Katie knows how to avoid paying interest and fees because of years of working in banks. Having students meet Katie is always my favorite session because she shows them how to save tons of money without hardly lifting a finger. Her husband, Bart, who happens to be a good friend of mine, thinks she is a compulsive shopper and wonders why in the world I would ever let her near my students. What he doesn't understand is that as long as her Vital Signs stay positive and she is working toward her goals, it doesn't matter how she chooses to spend *her* money.

As I was thinking about Katie at Java Road, Cindy and her brother Brent joined me and informed me that Scott was under the weather. I quickly asked Brent some questions and did my best to form a diagnosis. What I learned, in a nutshell, is that Brent has two things going for him financially—he owns a home and he makes a decent salary. I also learned that he is a compulsive shopper, an eccentric day-trader, and on the verge of losing his house because of all his debt.

Katie stormed into Java Road with her usual swagger. "I heard you over there talking about Vital Signs, Dr. Dink. I thought you'd be proud to know that I'm about to buy a new Jaguar and I can still meet my savings goals *and* keep my Vital Signs positive."

"I don't know how you do it, Katie."

"Of course you do. I do it by working my tush off. I've been putting in some hundred-hour weeks since I got this promotion, and I'm loving every minute of it."

"Work hard, shop hard—nothing has changed, right, Katie?" I said.

"And it isn't going to change. Speaking of which, I need to swing by the mall. Why don't you two look over this list while I go make a quick phone call." Katie excused herself from the table and handed Cindy and Brent a piece of paper.

Katie's Rules for Smart Banking

1. Don't pay fees for basic banking services such as check writing.
2. Choose a bank that requires only a low—or preferably no—minimum balance.
3. Pay your bills on time to avoid late fees, don't bounce checks, and don't go below your required balance.
4. Check your bank and credit card statements as if they are filled with gold, and be sure you can account for all the charges. Billing mistakes almost always go against you.
5. Contest incorrect charges, late fees, and interest payments. Just call and ask the bank to have them removed.
6. Choose a bank that offers free ATM transactions and a large network of ATM machines, so you don't have to pay an unnecessary fee from another bank's machine.

When Katie returned to the table, we all walked out to Katie's Mercedes and Katie got right to business. "To implement these suggestions, a good place to start is your company's credit union. Credit unions are often set up as a service to employees and thus offer low fees and excellent rates. If your company doesn't have one, you can do fine by going to a bank, but just be sure to sign up for the right account. Most banks—the good ones, anyway—will take the time to walk you through the benefits of each type of account."

The purpose of Katie teaching this session was to show my students that good financial health means that you should enjoy the money you earn. Too many students get the impression that the key to financial success is never to spend any money. What I wanted Cindy to learn, and obviously to pass on to Scott, was that if you can eliminate unnecessary bank fees and interest, you will be able to put that money toward the things that bring you pleasure.

On the way to the mall, Katie stopped by the vet to check on her beloved cat. Just as she did with herself, Katie spared no expense when it came to her little Patches. Whether it was for holidays or just any old occasion, Katie loved that she didn't have to worry too much when it came to spoiling those who were close to her, and Patches was near the top of that list.

After a short drive, we arrived at the mall and Katie could hardly contain herself. With a pocketbook full of dough, Katie was armed and ready to start spending some of her hard-earned cash. As she bounced from store to store, buying a skirt here and a blouse there for herself, a book for a coworker, a toy for Patches, and a nine-iron for her husband Bart, she continued her discussion on banking.

"Regardless of whether you have a credit union, you should still research at least three banks. After you've chosen your bank, they may ask that you do two things, and you should readily accept both of them. The first will be to use direct deposit. This is to your benefit, since the money goes into your account the day you get paid and it saves you from having to make the deposit yourself. The second is to use ATM machines for transactions, which is faster for you anyway. The banks do this because it saves them money on labor, which allows them to pass on the savings to you. Besides, you probably have better things to do than stand on line at the bank."

At this point, the four of us were sitting on one of those uncomfortable mall benches, and Katie said, "Now it's time to fork over your bank statements, Cindy."

"You're not going to like them," Cindy said as she handed them to Katie.

"Monthly maintenance fee—$7; insufficient funds—$25! There's dinner for two that you just gave to the bank—enough to drive Dr. Dink mad. Is this the norm?" Katie asked.

"To be honest, Katie, I don't pay much attention to my statements," Cindy replied, a little worried about the stern look on Katie's face.

"Assuming this is an average month, you are spending $384 a year on bank charges," said Katie, who seemingly had a calculator in her head. "How many new outfits is that?"

"I see your point, Katie. But apparently you haven't heard of Dr. Dink's motto: 'Don't Preach—Teach.'"

"Well, I have a motto, too, and it's 'Enjoy the Money You Earn,'" Katie said. "Spending money is one thing, but when you lose money out of sheer laziness, by forgetting to make a payment on time or by getting a bank fee for a bounced check, you are simply taking away the chance to buy something that will make you feel good. Right now, the bank is the one enjoying the money you earn. Would you prefer it that way?"

Cindy was speechless after Katie's question, as was I, since I was thinking about how much I liked Katie's motto. I can live with students who have a tendency to overspend, but it's the waste that drives me crazy. Things like parking tickets, late fees, $300 phone bills, and bounced checks suck money out of the Vital Signs and return nothing but frustration. Brent interrupted my thoughts and asked, "What about the concept of floating money on credit cards?"

"Great idea," said Katie, "as long as you don't have an outstanding balance and you pay the bill on time. There are huge fees when you pay a credit card late—sometimes they even freeze your credit card, and we all know how embarrassing a frozen card can be."

"I'm not saying to pay late," Brent explained. "I'm just talking about floating money by timing the dates when your credit card bills are due."

Brent was definitely slick, but based on his debt, he was obviously too slick for his own good. Not surprisingly, Katie knew what he meant by "floating money" and responded with a perfect example. She said, "My friend Brad often makes big purchases on the twenty-second of any given month, since his billing cycle ends on the twenty-first. For example, if he buys a $3,000 stereo on May 22, the charge will appear on his June 21 statement, and then his payment isn't actually due until July 21. Therefore, he gets an interest-free loan for almost two months. He's smart, but more important, he's organized. Very few people have the time and discipline to pull this off."

"That's what I tried to do," said Brent, "but I never really kept track of things and I always thought I had more money than I did."

"It's easy to keep track if you're organized," said Katie, "and if—"

"I know," interrupted Cindy, "you can't have any credit card debt to begin with."

"Which brings me back to your personal credit card debt," said Katie. "Let's start with the basics. There are only two steps to get out of debt. The first one is to *save enough money to pay off your balances with cash.* And the other way is to *lower your interest rate.* Paying off the balance is a function of your Vital Signs, and it's up to you to find that money in your budget. Lowering your interest rate takes some work—but not that much work. And wouldn't you know it, I have a list I prepared on that very same topic."

Katie's Keys to Low-Interest Debt—
From Least Work to Most Work

1. Call your bank or credit card company and simply ask for a lower rate.
2. Transfer your debt to a credit card with a lower fixed rate or a teaser rate.
3. Apply for a loan with your bank, employer, or credit union.
4. Work out a loan with a friend or family member.
5. If you own a home, obtain a home equity loan.
6. Arrange a meeting with a consumer credit counseling agency.
7. As a last resort, consider declaring personal bankruptcy.

"Call your current creditors and ask for a lower rate," said Cindy as she studied the list. "It sounds too easy."

And it is too easy, I thought. But it works. One of the reasons I was able to get out of $25,000 worth of credit card debt is that I always called my creditors and asked for a lower rate, and nine times out of ten, they agreed. The industry is so competitive that as long as I made my minimum payments, my creditors were happy to keep my business by lowering my rate. It's just another example that those who ask for a better price usually get it.

Katie interrupted my thoughts and said, "The next idea is to transfer balances to a card with a lower interest rate, and there are a few ways to do this. One is to take advantage of teaser rates such as an introductory rate of 3.9 percent for six months. Then, in six months, you can transfer the remaining balance to another card with a teaser rate."

This was another technique that I used, and it can be a little tricky. The credit card companies like to "suck you in" with a low rate, often called a teaser rate, and then hope that you forget when the "introductory" period ends. Usually, the rate jumps to 20 percent and most consumers don't even pay attention. It's not so much that the creditors are unethical—they are simply preying on human nature. But for those who are organized, taking advantage of these low rates can be a great way to reduce your interest cost.

Katie continued: "Another approach is to find a low fixed rate of around 9.9 percent and not worry about all the hassle of changing cards. Paying an annual fee of no more than $50 is not so bad if you can reduce your monthly interest rate. The combination approach is to take advantage of a teaser rate, and then when that expires, call the creditor and negotiate a low fixed rate. Credit card companies don't like losing interest-paying customers who pay their bills on time."

I was getting a little concerned that Katie was dominating the conversation and Cindy and Brent were turning into spectators, and then finally Cindy spoke. "What about number four, work out a loan with a friend or family member? That sounds like trouble to me!" exclaimed Cindy. "Money ruins relationships, ends friendships, and breaks up families."

"You're right on all three counts, Cindy, and if you are not comfortable with borrowing money from your family, then don't do it," said Katie. "But one way to make it work is to structure the loan so that it's a good deal for both parties. Suppose your parents are conservative investors and are earning 5 percent on their current investments and you are paying 20 percent on your loans. Offer to pay them somewhere in the middle so you both win. They get a better return on their 'investment' and you get a much lower interest rate. As long as you pay your bills on time, it's a win-win situation."

In this case, I thought Cindy and Katie had both made excellent points. Mixing family and money is often a recipe for a disaster, unless it can truly become win-win.

Although he was quiet, Brent apparently was taking all this in, because he said, "I can see the virtues of asking for a loan, but I don't know about going to my boss. What do you mean by taking out an installment loan with my employer?" Brent asked.

Katie handled this one. "Many companies offer loans or give cash advances as a service to their employees. If they provide the service, then you shouldn't feel bad about taking advantage of it. That's what it's there for—so the employees can use it if they feel they need to."

"I had no idea such a thing even existed," Cindy said. "I'll check into that one as well. What else is there?"

At this point, I was really glad Brent came along because he is a homeowner and I knew he would be a prime candidate for this. I explained rule five. "A home equity loan is similar to a mortgage in that it gives you a low rate and the interest payments are tax deductible. It is nothing more than a loan, reserved for homeowners, which usually carries a low interest rate. Forgive me, Brent, because I'm not that familiar with your situation, but why haven't you considered a home equity loan in the past?"

"My house is my most prized possession," said Brent. "I don't want the bank owning any more of it than they already do."

I could understand this response since I heard it so often. There is something about owning a house that gives people peace of mind, and it's not surprising when students get touchy about a loan that involves using their house as collateral. What most people forget, however, is that a mortgage uses their home as collateral as well.

When Brent insisted that he was against it, Katie laid into him. "Brent, if you are paying 20 percent interest on your credit cards and you are in debt up to your ears, they're going to take your house soon enough! Home equity loans are typically around the prime rate, which is about 9 percent right now. And just like your mortgage payment, your home equity payments are tax-deductible. In other words, you typically get a lower interest rate and gain a tax benefit when you take out a home equity loan. Let me show you an example. How much high-interest debt are you carrying and what is the interest rate?"

"About fifteen grand when you add up all the department store loans and credit cards, and the average rate is about 20 percent. Cindy has about the same."

"I see you and your sister have more in common than just big ears," teased Katie. "Let me break out the old calculator here and show you something."

After a few minutes, Katie produced the following table:

Amount of Debt	Interest Rate	Annual Interest and Principal Payments	Total Cost of Debt Over Ten Years
$15,000	20%	$3,480	$34,800
$15,000	14%	$2,796	$27,960
$15,000	11%	$2,484	$24,840
$15,000	7%	$2,088	$20,880

"Do you really think I can get a 7 percent loan?" asked Cindy.

"No, but I wouldn't be surprised if your brother can," Katie answered. "For a home equity loan, the interest rate is a function of your income, credit history, and the equity in your house. I tried to be conservative by saying 9 percent, which brings the *real rate,* meaning after the tax write-off, closer to 7 percent. Remember that the interest you accrue on the loan is tax-deductible—just like a mortgage. So assuming Brent can get 9 percent, his real rate would be about 7 percent. That's what I show in the bottom column."

I wasn't sure if Cindy and Brent understood what Katie meant when she said "real rate." Just as I had explained in the lecture at ASU, the interest on mortgage payments as well as home equity payments is tax-deductible. So, when the tax savings are factored in, a rate of 9 percent is more like a rate of 7 percent. Apparently, Katie did a good enough job of explaining this, because Cindy and Brent both seemed charged up.

"Think about all you can do with the $14,000 you will be saving," said Cindy, who was pretty quick at math in her own right. She was indeed right that the difference between a rate of 20 percent and 7 percent was almost fourteen grand—an eye-popping figure.

"There are a lot of different ways to approach this," Katie started in again. "I am struggling with your situation, Brent, because I did not get a complete diagnosis from Dr. Dink. You could make higher payments if you wanted to pay the loan off faster or you could use the extra money to invest. That would be up to you."

"Tell me about that option," said Brent. "I love to day-trade stocks."

"That's between you and your Finance Doctor," said Katie. "But as I'm sure he has told Cindy time and time again, your best investment is paying off high-interest debt. I wouldn't even think about investing until you have paid that amount off. And as far as day trading goes, I've read reports that 99 percent of day traders lose money."

Brent's comment about day trading as well as Brooke's comment during the lecture at ASU about Internet stocks going up 300 percent were two examples of why financial therapy is an 8-step process. Uneducated students, who read only the headlines, often hear about a person or a handful of people who have gotten rich quick in the stock market. What they don't understand is that all investments carry risks and the ones that go through the roof are also the ones that, more often than not, end up going bankrupt.

I was thankful to have Katie around to do my dirty work. Her table on the home equity loan was a perfect example to highlight the impact of getting a lower rate. And even though Cindy probably didn't have a chance to get a rate as low as 7 percent, the difference between 11 percent interest and 20 percent interest on $15,000 worth of debt was still about ten grand over ten years. I wanted to make sure that Cindy was still involved, so I said, "Now let's get back to Cindy."

"Can I leave now?" asked Brent. "I want to make some trades before the markets open in Asia."

"Sure, but before you get that home equity loan, be sure to do plenty of research and use the Buyer's Antibiotic—get three bids before you do anything," said Katie, sounding a little too much like me.

"I don't need to do that," said Brent. "I'm going to use the guy my neighbor used."

"But, Brent, how do you know if your neighbor got a good deal?" asked Katie.

"Gotta go, Katie, thanks for the tips," said Brent as he sprinted out of the mall as if he knew exactly what time the next bus was coming. I was disappointed that Brent seemed interested only in freeing up extra cash to make risky investments, and showed no signs of being committed to a lifetime of sound financial health. The reason I didn't try to stop him from leaving was that I have learned over the years that those who are successful in financial therapy are the ones committed to change. Although Brent did not fit that bill, it was nice to know that he was at least willing to get a home equity loan and take money out of the credit card companies' hands to enjoy for himself. And because Cindy had learned a valuable lesson about home equity loans, the time was well spent. Staring at the chart, Cindy finally said, "What kind of rate do you think I can get?"

"Unfortunately, I have no idea without seeing your credit history," said Katie. "Listen, I still have a few things to return at Neiman Marcus and then Saks Fifth Avenue. Why don't I meet you two in front of Saks in twenty minutes."

Since neither Cindy nor I had any business spending money in this fancy mall, we decided to get some air and talk about what she had learned so far. Cindy confided in me that she had never seen a person seem so carefree with money and at first wondered why I had introduced Katie to her. Then, to my delight, she told me that she had remembered something I had said to her during our first meeting at Java Road: *A successful student is one who meets the goals that they have outlined.*

I wanted to show her that as long as you make more money than you spend *and* you are meeting your goals, you don't need to worry too much about how you spend money. I don't look down on those who enjoy spending money on material things. Because Katie worked at a bank, she was the perfect person to exemplify how to take money out of the pockets of the banks and creditors and enjoy it yourself.

Full of enthusiasm, Cindy said to me, "Listen, Doc, I've been inspired by Katie, and I especially love her motto—'Enjoy the Money You Earn.' While this stuff is still fresh in my head, I want to get right to work on the things Katie talked about. Can we finish up this session tomorrow?"

"Sounds good to me," I said. "We'll go over the last two rules at Java Road and then you can go and do your homework."

When we met up with Katie in front of Saks, not surprisingly, she could barely carry all her packages. "I thought you had a few things to *return*," said Cindy.

"I did, but I found a few things I couldn't pass up. Listen, I need to hustle back to work. If you don't mind, I'll drop you back at Java Road."

We arrived back at Java Road, and before sending Cindy on her way, I still had to address the last two items on Katie's list, starting with "Arrange a meeting with a consumer credit counseling agency." Consumer credit counselors provide assistance to people dealing with stressful financial situations. I said to Cindy, "The way it works is that you agree to make one payment each month to the organization, which in turn sends payment to your individual creditors. The primary benefit is that you will lower the overall cost of your debt, because of reduced or waived finance charges that the agency has negotiated for you. When you have completed your payments, they will help you reestablish credit."

Cindy had apparently heard about these agencies, but she was afraid that they might hurt her credit report. It was kind of an ironic statement, considering that she already told me that she couldn't get approved for any more credit cards. I explained, "While some people are afraid that going to a consumer credit agency is a black mark on their credit report, what they don't realize is that without this step, many people have no chance of repairing their credit. I have students who have enrolled in these programs and have been able to obtain a mortgage upon completing their payment cycle. Another benefit of these agencies is that they sponsor educational programs on topics such as buying a house and teaching kids about money."

I encouraged Cindy to at least stop by the agency in her area to learn more. I also wanted to discuss the last of Katie's rules—the one concerning bankruptcy—before I sent Cindy on her way. I started by reading her a quote from Terry Savage, an award-winning journalist: "Bankruptcy does not wipe your credit slate clean and give you a fresh start. Bankruptcy should be a last resort to solving financial problems—when the mountain of debt is so great and the creditors so unrelenting that no other accommodation can be reached."

In 1999, 1.3 million bankruptcies were filed, and 97 percent of those were filed by individuals, not businesses. My goal is to prevent my students from having to resort to bankruptcy. I said to Cindy, "Bankruptcy stays on your credit report for ten years and is not the 'quick fix' that it is often made out to be. Let's hope that's all you'll ever need to know."

After going through all of Katie's points, Cindy finally made it home and got right to work.

Exercise 5A

Perform all the appropriate steps from Katie's list.

**Katie's Keys to Low-Interest Debt—
From Least Work to Most Work**

1. Call your bank or credit card company and simply ask for a lower rate.
2. Transfer your debt to a credit card with a lower fixed rate or a teaser rate.
3. Apply for a loan with your bank, employer, or credit union.
4. Work out a loan with a friend or family member.
5. If you own a home, obtain a home equity loan.
6. Arrange a meeting with a consumer credit counseling agency. Call the National Foundation for Consumer Credit at 1-800-388-2227, or visit their Web site at www.nfcc.org.
7. As a last resort, consider declaring personal bankruptcy. You can contact the American Bankruptcy Institute at 703-739-0800, or visit their Web site at www.abiworld.org.

Meanwhile . . . Back at Java Road the Next Day

While I was waiting for Cindy at Java Road, I finally had time to look over her exercises from the previous week. She had mentioned that she had $15,000 in high-interest debt, but I never got the chance to look it over. It was fairly typical, and it was enough to almost bring a Finance Doctor to tears. I decided to look on the positive side, and reasoned that it gave us tremendous opportunity for improvement.

Results from Cindy and Scott's Exercise 4

Creditor	Type	Interest Rate	Balance
Visa	Credit card	18.9%	$3,000
MasterCard	Credit card	19.9%	$2,500
Department store	Credit card	21.9%	$1,700
Appliance store	Credit card	22.5%	$4,800
Department store	Credit card	18.9%	$3,000

Just as I finished reading it over, Cindy sat down at my booth and seemed excited. "Good news all around, Doc," she said. "I went to my credit union and found out that I can get free checking with no minimum-balance requirement. There's $32 a month that I'll be saving, and it gets even better. I also qualified for a $5,000 loan from the credit union at 13 percent because I've been with the company for five years. They weren't crazy about my debt-income ratio, as they called it, but I got the loan anyway."

"It sounds like you had a great resource there all along," I said. "I'm glad Katie pointed you in the right direction."

"She sure did, and speaking of which, I bit the bullet and talked to my parents. There was no way I could tell them that I have fifteen grand worth of debt, so I just told them I wanted to work out a loan for $5,000. They were going to write me a check, but I insisted on paying interest. Believe me, it's worth it to pay them interest so I don't have to worry about them holding the money over my head. We eventually settled on 6 percent. And then I called two of my credit card companies and they agreed to lower my rates from 18.9 percent and 19.9 percent to 14 percent, since I always make my payments on time. I'm now ready for some good news, Doc. How'd I do?"

I went to work on my calculator and said, "With three loans of $5,000 each at 6 percent, 13 percent, and 14 percent, your average rate is 11 percent. So instead of paying $3,480 a year in interest and principal, you have reduced it to $2,484. That's a monthly savings of $83."

"What about the savings in bank fees?" asked Cindy.

"It's great to know that you are going to save $384 a year by avoiding bank fees, but we can't show the improvement in your Vital Signs because we never had it in the Vital Signs to begin with. But it's always nice to plug a leak."

"It sure is," said Cindy. "I actually took the time to go through my old bank statements, and I had a lot of these fees—I can't believe how wasteful I've been. It's good to know that I'm not throwing away money anymore. And it's also comforting to have a credit union in my building at work so I can pay bills right there in person if I have to."

"You made a lot of progress in this session," I said. "I'll have to call Katie and thank her."

As Cindy and I sat in Java Road, I knew I was beaming—thinking about how much I loved my job. With just a little education and four phone calls—two to her credit card companies, one to her parents, and one to her credit union, Cindy and Scott would now be able to put $1,000 into their pockets each year—money that had previously been going to the banks. They were well on their way to living Katie's motto—Enjoy the Money You Earn.

Preparing for Next Week

With all this momentum, I knew Cindy would be excited about doing her exercises. I said to her, "Your exercise for next week is something I call '3-6-3,' and the numbers stand for ideas. The first 3 represents three ways you can improve inflows in your Vital Signs. For example, you can ask for a raise, work overtime, or start a small business on the side. The 6 represents six ideas to reduce outflows—things like lowering your phone bill or getting rid of your cell phone. And the last 3 represents three other lifestyle changes you can make that could improve either your inflows or outflows. Don't even worry about the numbers, we'll do that in our next session."

"Sounds great, Doc. I'll see you with Scott on Monday," said Cindy. "Same Bat-time, same Bat-place?"

"Actually, let's meet at your town house," I said. "This session is really about you and Scott making lifestyle changes to make sure that you make more than you spend every month. My mom has volunteered to work with you, and she's not much for coffee shops, but she loves to make house calls. She is a master of the Vital Signs and an avid practitioner of Q-Q-Kachoo. I've never seen a person get more for less than my mom. You can call her Erl—short for Erlaine."

Exercise 5B: 3-6-3

List 3 Ways to Improve Your Inflows (for example, asking for a raise or working a second job)

1.

2.

3.

List 6 Ways to Improve Your Outflows (for example, reducing your spending on clothes, eating out, and phone calls)

1.

2.

3.

4.

5.

6.

List 3 Creative Ideas to Improve Your Vital Signs (for example, working part-time at a school that gives free tuition to its employees)

1.

2.

3.

Chapter 6

Monitor Your Vital Signs— Make More Than You Spend

Too many people spend money they haven't earned, to buy things they don't want, to impress people they don't like.

—Will Rogers

If I had to put my finger on when I started thinking about money, it was probably at Mother's Pizza, where my mom would often take us on Monday nights when I was just a kid. It was my favorite night of the week because I loved pizza—still do—but I always wondered why we *only* went on Monday nights. Why not Friday night or Saturday night, when I didn't have to get up for school the next day? I was just eight years old when I asked my mom, "How come we only go out for pizza on Monday nights?"

My mom, who always knew a bargain when she saw one, looked me in the eye and said, matter-of-factly, "Because it's half-price night. To tell you the truth, I can't understand why anyone would come here any other night."

She also couldn't understand why anyone would walk into a department store and pay a marked-up price to buy a Polo shirt or a pair of Nike sneakers when it was only an hour's drive to the discount outlet stores in West Virginia. By making the extra effort to save a few dollars here and there, my mother was able to provide for me and my brother—and teach us a lesson about personal finance at the same time. In fact, most of my mom's friends—other single parents—were wizards when it came to personal finance, and to this day they remain my best teachers. Whether it was Bo renting out her basement for a few extra bucks, Valerie selling cosmetics to all her friends, or Sarah shoving Sweet'n Low packets in her purse whenever she went to a restaurant, this group always found a way to make ends meet.

That's why my mom was the best person to teach Cindy and Scott about making more money than they spent. She liked doing it as much as I liked the results, and no matter what, we always had a lot of fun together.

"I hope next week's homework is this easy," said Cindy as my mom and I entered Cindy and Scott's town house. "Here are my 3-6-3 results."

"Glad to see you are so anxious to get to work," said Erl, "but before we go over the results, let me state up front that financial therapy is really simple. I've never studied this stuff in school, but I learned through the school of hard knocks. The most important thing you can do is make good decisions. And that's why I cooked up these seven elements that will influence your financial health."

Erl's Seven "Hows" of Financial Health

1. How much you make.
2. How much you spend.
3. How much goes out for interest, fees, and taxes.
4. How you make decisions for major purchases.
5. How much you invest.
6. How long you invest the money.
7. How you invest the money.

"Today, we will only touch on the first two and I'll leave the rest of the work to my son, good old Dr. Dink," said Erl. "Our goal is to improve your Vital Signs, which is influenced by what two things?"

"What goes in and what goes out," answered Scott.

"Right. And when it comes to improving the Vital Signs, it is essential to look at the big picture," said Erl. "Most financial gurus just tell you to spend less and to deny yourself unnecessary services. What they forget to ask is whether income is fixed or variable."

"Hey, we didn't take any business classes, Erl. What the heck are you talking about?" asked Scott.

I decided to take this one, so I said, "Let me put it in simple terms. My friend Fred always makes a fixed salary, regardless of his performance. No matter how he performs at work, he gets his paycheck every two weeks, and each time it is for the same exact amount. On the other hand, as a salesman, his brother Vince's pay is based strictly on his performance. If he has a good week, his check is bigger. If he has a bad week, he better have some money in reserve.

"Fred used to tell Vince that he was wasting $240 a year by wearing dry-clean-only shirts. Fred also bragged that he saved by changing his own oil, washing his own car, and doing his own yard work. But all along, when he was telling Vince to do the same, he was giving him bad advice."

Cindy and Scott looked a little confused, and thankfully, Erl bailed me out. "The point is that you must determine if you have more time than money. *Don't bother clipping coupons to save two bucks if you could use that hour to make two hundred or two thousand.* Granted, Fred may have retired at age sixty with all that money he saved, but since Vince's income, as a commissioned salesman, is variable—not fixed—his time is better spent in front of customers than in his laundry room. As the old saying goes, sometimes you got to spend a little to make a little."

"Point taken, Erl, and in our case, our inflows are basically fixed," said Cindy. "So I guess all those fancy clothes are not really an investment. Since my income is fixed, they are more of an expense."

I was impressed that Cindy had remembered this lesson. Erl made Cindy feel good about it when she said, "Not if you and Scott see value in wearing nice clothes. I do not try to put a dollar figure on everything because it's impossible to put a dollar figure on everything. If wearing nice clothes makes you feel good or could lead to a promotion, or sets an example for your kids, then by all means don't eliminate nice clothes from your budget."

I'm glad that Cindy and Scott had a chance to warm up to Erl, and I was grateful that she gave such a good explanation on the differences between fixed and variable income. At this point, we were ready to get down to business, so I said, "Let's get back to the first part of your exercises. What are your three ideas for improving your inflows?"

"Ask my boss for a raise," said Cindy. "Have Scott ask his boss for a raise. And, number three, have the kids start modeling for cash. They're just adorable. Do you want to see pictures?"

"I'm not the one who gives out modeling jobs," said Erl. "By now, you know how to figure out if it's worth it—*Q-Q-Kachoo!* You have to find out what it costs to put together a portfolio, and then see how much time it will take and how much gas it will burn to go to all those agencies and see what they are paying. I was going to do this for my baby boy here, but he just wasn't that handsome. His brother, Andy, on the other hand—"

"Enough already, Erl," I interrupted, as the thought of Rogaine popped into my head. I was glad Erl reinforced Q-Q-Kachoo and validated Cindy's modeling idea, but I wanted to get something more concrete. "Back to inflows," I said. "Erl and I put together a list of ways you can improve them. I gave you the exercises to get your mind thinking in that direction."

Erl's Ways to Improve Inflows

1. Work more hours.
2. Work overtime, weekends, or holidays to earn time and a half or double time.
3. Work for more money.
4. Determine your market value, and if you are underpaid, ask for a raise.
5. Look for a new job.
6. If you work on commission, give yourself a raise and go sell something.
7. Look for a "side" job, such as selling cosmetics or telemarketing from home.

"Keep in mind, I am not saying to do all of these things," said Erl, after Cindy and Scott had a chance to look over the list. "You should just do the ones that you know you can accomplish. Which of these seven options seems feasible to you?"

"I'm definitely not going to work more hours," Cindy said. "I don't spend enough time with the kids as it is, and my company doesn't pay time and a half, so that's out too. But Scott's company pays time and a half on the weekends, and he just started picking up two extra shifts a month."

"What about working for more money?" asked Erl.

"Neither of us works on commission, so we have fixed income, as you would say," Scott said. "I don't know my market value, but I suppose it wouldn't hurt to find out. How do I go about doing that, though?"

"That's easy," Erl said. "Just pick up the paper, call a headhunter, go on the Internet, talk to others in your field, or set up a few job interviews. Then find a new job or ask for a raise at your current job. Not knowing what you are worth is unthinkable in this job market."

"Let's move on, and we'll finalize the strategy at the end," I said. "Here are some ideas to help you increase your income."

Other Ways to Make More Money

1. Make money from one of your hobbies—selling art, sculpture, carpentry, knitting, writing, playing an instrument, et cetera.
2. Take a second job, perhaps one where you work from your home or a sales job in which you can work your own hours.
3. Respond to surveys, market research, or medical studies that pay fees.
4. Do neighborhood chores—cut your neighbors' lawns, baby-sit their kids on nights you stay home, house-sit when your friends go away, take care of their pets, et cetera.
5. Put your kids to work—their work does not have to be limited to the above.
6. Sell unnecessary things—have a yard sale, or list items in classifieds at work, the newspaper, or on the Internet.
7. Rent out a room in your house or apartment.

"You really don't expect us to do all of those things, do you?" asked Cindy.

"Cindy, you haven't been listening," said Erl. "Not only do I not *expect* you to do all of those things, I don't *want* you to do all of those things. I can't ask you to rent a room in your basement when you don't even have a basement! I just want you to pick a minimum of three things and see what happens. Chances are, you'll generate some extra income that can be used in a variety of ways."

Erl was clearly on a roll, and as much as I didn't want to stop her, I wanted to establish a little bit of structure. "Before we move on to the outflows of your Vital Signs, I just need to put three ideas on paper that will help you improve your inflows and the approximate value of each."

"Scott will work one eight-hour shift every other weekend," said Cindy. "He normally earns $12 an hour, so he'll make $18 an hour for that overtime shift. You do the math, Dr. Dink."

"All right, I will. Sixteen hours a month times eighteen dollars is $288. Let's subtract 25 percent for taxes. That leaves us with $216."

"Here is my second idea," said Cindy. "We usually like to stay home on Friday nights, so I figure we can baby-sit other kids in the neighborhood. The going rate is seven bucks an hour. We could probably handle two families for five hours on three Fridays out of the month, so the total income should be . . ."

"Seven bucks times five hours is $35. Times that by two for the two families you'd be baby-sitting for, and that comes to $70. Three times a month makes $210," said Erl.

"My third idea is to ask for a raise of fifty cents an hour," Cindy said. "How much is that?"

Erl took this one too. "Well, if you work forty hours a week, that's a hundred sixty hours per month for a total of $80. Subtract 25 percent for taxes and you're left with an extra $60 on your monthly check."

"I'm positive I can get the extra fifty cents an hour," Cindy said. "But in the meantime, I'm going to find out my market value and see if I can make even more money."

"Scott, why don't you ask for a raise?" asked Erl. "Remember, the squeaky wheel gets the grease."

"My boss is a tightwad, but I suppose I could ask," said Scott. "Let's not count on that, but I am going to find out my market value as well. Maybe I can find a new job that pays the same, but also offers tuition reimbursement. After Dr. Dink's lecture at the university, I'm really starting to think that's a good alternative."

"Great idea," said Erl. "People often forget to consider perks and add up the value when they are evaluating their compensation. What else?"

"Going down your list, there's not much else," said Cindy. "We don't have any hobbies that we can make money from, and we have a tough enough time doing our own chores, much less the neighbors'. Plus, I'm not doing any surveys or taking any needles to make extra cash."

"Fair enough, but what about a yard sale?" asked Erl, who had many of these herself when we were growing up. "I also have an idea about all the CDs you've got stacked up next to your stereo, but I'll get to that later."

Before we moved on, I wanted to write down our progress so far and wrote this down on a piece of paper:

Inflows	**Before Erl**
Take-home pay from jobs	$3,000
Other income	$0
Total inflows	$3,000

"And here is what it should look like now with all of your suggestions," said Erl, who seemed to enjoy the fact that I had been scribbling while she was yapping.

Inflows	**After Erl**
Take-home pay from jobs	$3,000
Cindy's raise—50 cents an hour	$60
Scott's 2 weekend shifts	$216
Friday night baby-sitting	$210
Total inflows	$3,486

"Well, that looks pretty good, doesn't it?" asked Erl without letting Cindy and Scott answer. "Now that we've figured out how to raise your income an additional $486, let's take a look at your outflows. How do you think you can save money each month? Give me six ideas," she said.

"For starters, I know our phone bill is out of control, and I have lots of ideas on how to reduce that," said Cindy. "The first is to switch our long-distance carrier. One long-distance carrier offered me $50 just to switch over, *and* they said they'd lower my rate to seven cents a minute instead of the fifteen cents I'm paying now. I'm also going to start making my long-distance calls on weekends, when the rate is reduced to only five cents a minute. Plus, I'm going to try to send more postcards and use e-mail more at work."

"Sounds aggressive, Cindy, and I like it," said Erl. "I myself am a long-distance whore."

"What!" exclaimed Scott. "You didn't just say what I think you said."

Yes she did, I thought. For some reason, Erl gets a kick out of saying that. Every time a long-distance company offers her money to switch companies, she does, and she has probably saved thousands over the years by doing this. We've all been called by those telemarketers and gotten those annoying pieces of junk mail, but most of us just don't bother. Because Erl is one of those people who have more time than money, she does this time and time again.

Erl didn't acknowledge Scott's comment and instead said, "Do you think you could cut your $120 long-distance bill in half?"

"I'm going to do better than that," said Cindy. "I'm going to cut the bill down to $50 a month. And then there are the cell phones we have. We don't need two, and Scott's contract is just about to expire, so we can get rid of his phone. I still wouldn't feel safe not having mine, especially with the kids. But if we get rid of Scott's, that's an additional sixty bucks a month we'll save."

"Chalk up $720 a year for getting rid of a cell phone," I said, and then added, "What else can you come up with? What about your cable TV?"

"I figure we can do without the movie channels we have," said Scott. "They're a premium service and we have to pay extra for them. Plus, the neighbors have most of the channels we have and my brother has a satellite dish, so we can always have one of them tape a movie for us if we want to see it. That would save us another thirty bucks right there."

"And then there's our dry cleaning," said Cindy. They were on such a roll that Erl and I didn't dare interrupt. "I think we can save another twenty bucks if I just iron our clothes instead. I know it's a pain to iron sometimes, but to save twenty bucks a month, it's worth the extra time. And if we're more careful with our grocery shopping—you know, look for sales, clip coupons, buy in bulk, go to the warehouses—we should be able to save 15 percent on groceries, which would save us about $80 per month."

Just as I had anticipated, once Erl and I got the ball rolling, Cindy and Scott took over. Cindy continued, "I'm not going to give up my shopping altogether, but maybe I can cut it down substantially—say, by a hundred bucks a month. Let's also not forget the savings we're going to get by switching our insurance coverage. Where do we stand after all that?"

After writing quickly, their outflows looked like this:

Expense	Previous	Revised	Savings
Long distance	$120	$50	$70
Cell phones	$120	$60	$60
Cable	$50	$20	$30
Dry cleaning	$50	$30	$20
Groceries	$520	$440	$80
Shopping	$280	$180	$100
From Previous Exercises			
Car insurance	$180	$140	$40
Medical insurance	$25	$0	$25
Life insurance	$25	$0	$25
Credit card payments	$290	$207	$83
Savings Subtotal			**$533**

"Great news," I said as my arm was about to fall off from all the writing. "You have reduced your spending by $533 and your quality of life has barely changed. You have not had to move, give up your cars, or any of the other luxuries you enjoy. The way I see it, you'll still be able to keep in touch with your out-of-town friends, you'll still have your cell phone to feel safe, and you'll eat the same quality of food. The only thing you've really given up is a hundred dollars' worth of shopping and hundreds of bad cable movies at your beck and call."

"We can live without those things, but we're still not there yet," said Scott.

"Okay, let's do some more numbers," I said, knowing that showing progress would keep Cindy and Scott focused. "When you first did your Vital Signs, you had a deficit of $1,220, and now, with added inflows of $486 and additional savings of $533, you have reduced your deficit by more than a grand. To be exact, your deficit now stands at $201. But don't worry, we still have some more work to do in this session. Let's move on."

"Before I forget," said Scott, "you mentioned something about all my CDs earlier. What did you mean by that? You're not going to make me stop buying them, are you?"

"I know you're not going to stop buying them, and I know you're not going to sell all the ones you have," said Erl. "But if you want to buy a new CD, you have to sell one that's already in your collection."

"Actually, that's not such a bad idea," said Scott. "I've got tons of CDs that I don't even listen to anymore. I can't even remember why I bought that Dexys Midnight Runners CD, but I've probably only listened to it twice—and only for that one song, 'Come On Eileen.' I guess I could always tape the ones I'm going to sell—this way, if I think I'll ever want to hear them again, at least I'll have them on cassette."

"Great idea, Scott," I said, "and while we're talking about getting rid of unnecessary stuff, I think it's about time I taught you the 'Shoe Rule' that my buddy John, who lives in New York City, imposed on his wife."

"You can stop right there," said Cindy. "The last thing I need is another man telling me that I buy too many shoes."

Since Erl was familiar with the rule, I let her explain. "The Shoe Rule actually doesn't prevent you from buying shoes. It's just like the CD suggestion. All it says is that if you want to buy a pair of shoes, you have to get rid of a pair. John invented it more to save closet space than to save money, but as it turned out, it did both.

Because his wife hated to part with a pair of old shoes, she ended up spending a lot less money on new ones."

Cindy didn't say anything, probably because it was tough to argue with the logic of the Shoe Rule. That was a good thing, because we were ready to move on. I said, "The way I see it, there are really only four things left that we can still reduce—child care, pets, eating out, and clothing."

"Let's start with pets," said Erl. "What do you do with your dog when you go away on vacation?"

"We can't afford to go on vacation," said Cindy. "If we go on a day trip or even an overnight, we usually bring Cocoa with us."

I knew this wasn't the answer Erl was looking for, but I knew what she was getting at, so I elaborated. "When I was working in Chicago, I was friends with a married couple who were both consultants and traveled all the time for work. They spent $30 per night to keep their dog in a kennel, and their average monthly bill was $600 a month."

"Six hundred dollars a month for a kennel!" Erl said, nearly shouting. "Do you know that over five years, six hundred dollars a month at 5 percent interest compounded monthly is $40,803," she said as she looked up from her calculator. "Forty grand is a nice chunk of change for a down payment on a house."

"I got an idea," said Cindy, interrupting Erl's rampage. "We'll start a little pet-sitting business. We won't advertise or anything, but we have a bunch of neighbors who travel for work and have pets, so there should be some money to be made. Of course, we'll charge a lot less than the kennels. And if we ever go away, we'll have one of our "clients" return the favor and watch Cocoa for us. I think we can make $100 a month."

Erl was satisfied with Cindy's solution, so she immediately turned her attention to the clothing columns. "Don't forget that we have different columns for clothing—one for basic clothing and the other for shopping goodies, and we already reduced the shopping column by $100."

"And that's not going to get any lower," said Cindy. "But I think the $150 for basic clothing is a little high. I have all these boxes of clothes for the kids that people have given me that I haven't even looked at. I'm starting to realize that it doesn't make a difference to the kids what they wear, and I could easily go broke trying to impress other people. And then for the other necessities, like socks and underwear, we are going to start shopping in discount stores, where you can get great deals."

"There's no sense making it unrealistic," said Erl, "but how much do you think you can reduce clothing necessities by?"

"Let's say $80," said Cindy. "And while we're on the subject of the kids, I think we can save some major dough on child care. My mom and my brother are always offering to watch the kids, but I rarely take them up on it. It's just easier to have a teenager from the neighborhood come over than to drive fifteen or twenty minutes. But I feel more comfortable with family, and my mom really enjoys the kids. Plus, I'm starting to see that I've been spending money on something that I can get for free and with better care."

"I wish all of Dr. Dink's students were this creative," said Erl. "How about a number?"

"Let's cut it in half," said Scott. "But don't get greedy and go after our eating-out budget, too."

"Eating out is one of the few pleasures that I think you should enjoy," said Erl, who thrived when it came to getting the best deal at restaurants. "The way restaurants work, you can get the same meal for less depending on when you go. Because most people eat dinner around seven or eight and usually go to restaurants on the weekends, prices are typically lower if you go earlier in the night or on a weekday."

"But the menus are always the same," said Scott.

"You're right that they don't change the prices, but they often have specials," said Erl. "Some restaurants will have half-price burgers on Monday nights, free dessert on Tuesdays, or early-bird specials every night of the week. The beauty of it is that you often get even better service since the restaurant isn't as busy at those times. Another way to save money is to use two-for-one coupons. Most cities have an 'Entertainment' book that offers two-for-one dinners at hundreds of restaurants. It's thirty bucks a year, but it probably ends up saving me thousands every year. You can also check your local paper for two-for-ones at any number of restaurants."

"I've been meaning to buy that 'Entertainment' book," said Scott, "because it has coupons for most of the restaurants where we normally eat anyway. I also like the idea of half-price nights since we hate dealing with crowds on the weekends. Of course, I could use a place with half-price drinks after an hour with you, Erl!"

"Speaking of alcohol," I said, "if you enjoy fine wine or spirits, my recommendation is that you enjoy them at home. Alcohol is marked up big-time in restaurants, so you're better off enjoying your favorite wine over a home-cooked meal. Or, even better, you can find a restaurant that allows you to bring your own booze."

"So how much can we save if we're smarter about when we eat out?" asked Scott.

"I think it's reasonable to save $25 a month without giving up anything. Let's check our progress again.

Expense	Previous	Current	Savings
Pets	$50	+50	$100
Clothing	$150	$70	$80
Child care	$280	$140	$140
Eating out	$100	$75	$25
CDs	$60	$20	$40
Savings Subtotal			**$385**

"There's $385 more in savings and you haven't given up a thing," said Erl.

Even without doing the math, I knew we had done enough to turn a deficit of $1,220 into a surplus. I said, "Congratulations! You have just turned a $1,220 monthly deficit into a surplus—truly remarkable."

I may have sounded a bit dramatic, but I meant it. This was only our fifth session of financial therapy, and we had already accomplished the most important part of financial health—making more than you spend every month. Somehow—motherly instinct, I suppose—Erl knew exactly what I was thinking and said to me, "I'm impressed. But the way you're smiling, you're going to need rotator cuff surgery if you keep patting yourself on the back. There is still work to be done."

Erl was right, and before we moved on, I wanted to be sure that Cindy and Scott felt comfortable with the changes they made to their Vital Signs. "How does it feel to be over the hump?" I asked.

"To be honest, it feels funny," said Cindy. "On one hand, it almost seems too easy. We haven't had to make any major lifestyle changes. Driving the kids to my mom's house more and the two extra shifts that Scott will have to work are the only two big changes, and even those two aren't that dramatic."

"Keep in mind, it's easy to make changes on paper—making them in life isn't always so easy," cautioned Mom.

"That's what worries me," said Scott. "But I didn't know it was this bad when we began. I also know that we want to have a house and give our kids a good education. There's no question that running a $15,000 deficit won't allow us to achieve those goals. I'm also worried that after all that work, there still isn't much room for error."

"Here's another list that might be able to save you a few extra bucks," said Erl as she pulled out a piece of paper from her purse.

Erl's Ways to Get More for Less

1. Buy clothes out of season and travel at off-peak times.
2. Go to outlet stores and buy in bulk.
3. Negotiate—nearly everything is negotiable, just ask.
4. Buy things used—yard sales, consignment shops, online, newspapers, et cetera.
5. Use coupons and buy things on sale.
6. Make presents instead of buying them.

As Cindy and Scott looked over Erl's note, I could see the confidence in their eyes. At one point, Scott said, "If you told me a month ago that we could bring our Vital Signs into positive territory without changing our lifestyle very much, I would have said you were crazy. It just goes to show you what a little time and common sense can do."

After they thanked Erl for all of her help, I told Cindy and Scott to pack a bag for a day trip to New York City. We were going to meet two of my favorite teachers—Dr. Lori and Darius—to talk about investing. We all decided to meet at Java Road before our flight. Fortunately, I had saved enough frequent-flyer miles from my days as a consultant that our flights were free. This was one field trip that I was happy to chaperone.

Exercise 6

Find out the value of your cars, major possessions worth more than $500, and all of your financial holdings.

Item	**Dollar Value**
Checking account	
Savings account	
Investments	
Cars	
Other	

Chapter 7

Keep Your Balance and Know the Rule of 72

You cannot be emotionally healthy without healthy attitudes toward money. If you are needy, you suffer. If you are greedy, you suffer.

—Dana Smith

In my family, it wasn't so much the *absence* of money that brought us closer together, as it was the notion that we had to work together in the present in order to meet our goals in the future. My dad, my brother, and I typically spent Friday nights in the laundry room at his apartment complex. Frugal, practical Dad reasoned that by laundering his own dress shirts, he would save about $20 a month in dry-cleaning expenses and since he had to wash all his other clothes anyway, it wasn't such a big deal. For my brother and me, it hardly seemed like work, and we certainly bonded more in that laundry room than we ever did in front of the TV playing video games.

What Andy and I didn't know at the time was what my dad was doing with the money he was saving—he was investing. All those issues of *Money* magazine and old copies of the *Wall Street Journal* that my dad kept in his office were not just for show. Every month, he invested a set amount in a mutual fund, with the goal of retiring before age sixty. While my dad would never tell us exactly how much he saved, I went back myself and did the numbers to see just how much his "investment" of laundering his own shirts turned out to be worth. In this case, doing the numbers was easy. Twenty dollars per month contributed to an IRA resulted in a mind-boggling savings of $110,000 and a one-way ticket to retirement in Florida at the tender age of fifty-eight!

As I often say, figures don't lie but liars figure, but in this case, there's no denying the miracle of compound interest. I had this story in mind when Cindy and Scott met me at Java Road. We had a flight to catch, so I got right to it. "I'm not going to bore you with much accounting, but today we have to talk about balance sheets. A balance sheet simply tells you where you stand at the moment. Think of it as a snapshot of your financial health, since it tells you what you have right now."

"Borrrr-ing," mocked Cindy.

I was a little afraid of this, since the mere mention of anything to do with accounting scares some people, but it was critical. I decided to start with a simple example for Cindy and Scott, and I said, "A balance sheet is like a résumé of your financial health that tells you what you have and who owns it. For example, if you own a house that is worth $150,000 and you have a mortgage for $125,000, the amount that you actually own is $25,000. The balance sheet would look like this."

Asset:		**Liability**	
House	$150,000	Mortgage	$125,000
		Owner's Equity	
		Your share	$25,000

I continued, "The reason that each side of the balance sheet always adds up is that for every asset, *someone* has to own it. It balances because for all your assets, either you are the owner or one of your lenders is the owner. In most cases, it is a combination of both.

In the example of the house, the bank owns $125,000 of the house and the $25,000 that is left belongs to the owner. The amount you owe to someone is called a liability. In this case, the mortgage is money owed to the bank, and then whatever is left over is yours—your owner's equity."

Before we left Java Road for the airport, I wanted to help Cindy and Scott put together a balance sheet, since it would be critical for them to know where they stood on the investment front. Just as I had expected, Cindy and Scott had done their exercises and had given me all the information I needed to create their balance sheet. It was relatively straightforward, and the only math I had to do was to multiply their monthly payments by the number of remaining payments to figure out the total liability for their student loans and their cars. For the student loans, they had sixty-four more payments at $150 each, so the liability was $9,600. After doing the same calculation for the car payments, it looked like this:

Cindy and Scott's Balance Sheet

Assets		**Liabilities**	
Cash/Checking	$500	Credit cards 14%	$5,000
Savings	$500	Credit union 13%	$5,000
Minivan	$10,000	Minivan 9%	$7,400
Convertible	$14,000	Convertible 9%	$8,000
Stocks, bonds, etc.	$0	Student loans 8%	$9,600
Retirement plans	$25,000	Personal loan 6%	$5,000
Total Assets	**$50,000**	**Total Liabilities**	**$40,000**
		Owner's Equity	**$10,000**

Total Assets:	**$50,000**
Total Liabilities:	**$40,000**
Owner's Equity: (Net worth)	**$10,000**

Cindy and Scott didn't really seem to know what to make of this balance sheet until I said, "The good news is that when we subtract your total assets from your total liabilities, we see that you have a net worth of ten thousand dollars."

"Greek islands, here we come!" said Cindy.

"Wait a second, not so fast. The bad news is that you don't have access to all those assets. To use Wall Street terms, just about all your assets are illiquid." Just as I said this, I knew that I would need to explain. A balance sheet does provide an inventory of assets, but often assets and cold cash are entirely two different things. I continued, "The money in your 401(k) is not money that you can spend right now. In fact, if you tried to liquidate it—in other words, turn it into cash—you would have to pay a huge penalty. Because you can't touch that money until you are 59½ without negative tax consequences and big penalties, you have to consider it illiquid."

Cindy and Scott seemed to understand this point, so I continued, "And while you could certainly liquidate your cars and turn those assets into cash, you would be left with nothing to drive. So when we look at your balance sheet, all but $1,000—the money in your checking and savings account—is illiquid."

One of the things that I hadn't explained was the percentages listed in the balance sheet. I said, "You'll notice that under liabilities, I have listed your liabilities in order—from highest interest rate to lowest. What you want to do is start by getting rid of the liabilities at the top."

"So in other words, Doc," said Cindy, "when we have extra money in our checking account, we should put it toward those credit cards at 14 percent. Katie told me that we should never have debts that carry an interest rate above 10 percent. I guess that means that once my 14 percent credit card bill is paid off, the credit union loan at 13 percent is next."

I was thrilled with Cindy's assessment. As is the case with most students, once they get into the 8 Steps, they start to make their own conclusions. "Any ideas on how to work off those liabilities?" I asked.

"It's tough, Doc," said Scott. "It seems like we have gotten to the point where our Vital Signs are about even, but it's not like there is extra money to pay off any of those balances. I feel good about our retirement account, but we haven't begun to address education, vacations, and everything else that we're going to encounter down the road."

Scott's point was a good one. There was no magic wand to get rid of those liabilities, and students sometimes get frustrated when there isn't a quick fix. I had to bring them back to basics. "Remember, the most important element in good financial health is your Vital Signs, which means you have to make more than you spend every month. Keep in mind that when we revised your Vital Signs, we included the monthly payments on these liabilities. As long as you keep making those payments and you don't add to your debt, the liabilities will start to decrease."

With a completed balance sheet and a firm understanding of how to improve it, we were just about ready to leave for the airport. Even though there are no quick fixes, I do like to recommend an old-fashioned housecleaning as a fast way to make a dent on the liabilities side of a balance sheet. Whenever I go through my belongings, three things inevitably happen. The first is that I'm able to make some money by selling things that I no longer need—an old computer or an old stereo that has since been upgraded. The second is that I end up with a pile of things to give for charity. This not only makes me feel good, but it also provides the added bonus of being a tax write-off. The third benefit is that I feel more organized and my life feels less cluttered. I can't put a dollar figure on it, but I know I always feel great after I do it.

I said to Cindy and Scott, "Why not have a yard sale and donate whatever is left over to charity? It will help you earn some cash, eliminate clutter, and make you feel good about giving to others."

"I don't mind selling some of that stuff, but we don't do yard sales," said Scott.

"Then sell it another way. You can put ads in the paper; you can post signs on bulletin boards; you can put it up for auction on the Internet. Or you probably can get rid of a bunch of stuff just by word of mouth."

"I'm definitely a pack rat," said Cindy. "I'm sure we have at least a thousand dollars' worth of stuff in our storage locker. I'll start liquidating."

When I heard Cindy using Wall Street lingo, I knew we were ready to venture to the Big Apple.

Airborne

On the plane, I explained to Cindy and Scott why we were going to New York. Dr. Lori, a Ph.D. in clinical psychology and a good friend of mine from Cornell, had an incredible knack for explaining the "human" side to investing. She understood that security and peace of mind were much more important than maximizing returns. Back when she was getting her Ph.D., she was struggling financially and came to me for help. This reinforced the fact that even some smart, well-educated people know nothing about finance. Even Dr. Lori, a brilliant woman, thought that Dow Jones was Jimmy Smits's replacement on *NYPD Blue.*

As it turned out, I learned as much from her as she learned from me. She shared much of her knowledge about psychology with me, which I ultimately incorporated into financial therapy. All the while, she gained a solid understanding of personal finance. Together, we made a great duo.

Dr. Lori had agreed to pick us up at the airport and transport us to our second teacher—Darius. Remember, Darius was the guy who, in one phone conversation, helped me create financial therapy and become Dr. Dink. He had now been working on Wall Street for six years, with an MBA from Stanford sandwiched in between.

When we landed in New York, Dr. Lori, all four feet ten inches of her, was there to meet us. We had a lot to cover in the drive from La Guardia Airport to Wall Street, and for a change, I was hoping for traffic. Dr. Lori started talking in her fast-paced New York accent. “I have a Ph.D. in psychology, and the reason Dr. Dink asked me to talk to you is that money is as much about psychology as it is about finance. For example, the best motivation to invest is to see where your investment is taking you. It’s the reason why Dr. Dink insists that you start financial therapy by creating your vision of financial wellness. Before you get into the details about investing, I think you should see what outcome you are trying to achieve.”

I knew Dr. Lori was setting Cindy and Scott up for the Rule of 72, and she was doing so perfectly. When I first learned this rule, it changed the way I thought about investing, and I knew it would for Cindy and Scott as well. She continued, “*The most significant factor in investing is how long you invest your money.* You will see what I mean after I teach you the Rule of 72. It’s always where I like to start.”

I had a prescription card handy:

The Finance Doctor

℞

THE RULE OF 72

Divide 72 by your rate of return to see how long it will take to double your money.

Dr. Dink, MBA

"I don't get what you mean by rate of return," said Cindy, displaying the patience of a New Yorker. I let Dr. Lori explain. "For example, let's say you earn a return of 12 percent when you invest your money. Divide 72 by 12 and you get 6. So you will double your money every six years."

"I think where you are losing us is when you say 'rate of return,'" said Scott, and I was glad he had raised this point again.

"It's the amount of interest you earn on your investment," said Dr. Lori. "If you keep your money in a savings account that offers a rate of 4 percent annual interest, your rate of return is simply 4 percent. After one year, $1,000 would have earned $40 in interest—a rate of 4 percent."

I still wanted to clarify one thing, so I said, "Keep in mind, your return on investment doesn't just mean interest. If you took that same $1,000 and bought a stock, and at the end of a year it was worth $1,100, your rate of return would be 10 percent. The amount your investment goes up—or appreciates, as they say on Wall Street—is your rate of return."

Dr. Lori got back to work and asked, "If your rate of return is 8 percent, how long will it take to double your money?"

Cindy answered. "Seventy-two divided by eight is nine, so we will double our money every nine years. What if we only earn 2 percent, Scott?" Cindy asked, playing right along with Dr. Lori's way of teaching.

"Then we will double our money every thirty-six years," answered Scott. "But on the other hand, if we earn 36 percent, we will double our money every two years. This rule really makes sense."

It was no surprise that Dr. Lori, a big fan of visuals, had a chart prepared for Cindy and Scott to reference.

Rule of 72

Annual Rate of Return	Years It Takes to Double Money
2%	36
4%	18
6%	12
8%	9
12%	6
18%	4
24%	3

Dr. Lori kept on going. "Keep in mind that the Rule of 72 is the same whether you are the lender or the borrower. So if you are paying 18 percent interest and just let your debt sit there without making any payments, how long will it take for your debt to double?"

"Seventy-two divided by 18 is four years," said Cindy. Four years to double your debt, I thought to myself. At this rate, sixty million Americans will have $14,000 worth of credit card debt in four years, instead of the average of $7,000 that they have right now. The power of compound interest is a double-edged sword. It can grow your debt as quickly as it can grow your savings. And for those who pay 18 percent or more on their credit cards, the debt grows a heck of a lot more quickly than the savings do.

While I was thinking, Dr. Lori kept teaching: "Taking it a step further, if you have $10,000 of debt at 18 percent, and don't make any payments on it, how much debt will you have in twelve years?"

"After four years, it will be $20,000," said Cindy, who was counting on her fingers at this point. "After eight years, it will be $40,000. And after twelve years it will be $80,000. And after sixteen years—I better get some extra credit—it will be $160,000."

"The actual amount is $174,373," said Dr. Lori, who had taken her preparation seriously. "The reason that the actual amount is higher is that the credit card companies calculate interest monthly. All you really need to know is that every fancy technique those credit card companies use takes more and more money out of your pocket."

"Now I know why it's so hard to get out of debt," said Scott. "I want the Rule of 72 to start working for us and not against us. So when are you going to tell us how to earn 18 percent on our money?"

Scott's response was just what I was looking for. Dr. Lori had not only explained the Rule of 72 perfectly, but had also reinforced just how punishing credit card debt can be. After handing Scott and Cindy another piece of paper, Dr. Lori continued, "Right now you have $25,000 in your 401(k). Let's look at how much that will be worth in thirty-six years when you're ready to retire."

Annual Rate of Return	Years to Double Money	Value of $25,000 in 36 Years
2%	36	$50,000
4%	18	$100,000
6%	12	$200,000
8%	9	$400,000
12%	6	$1,600,000
18%	4	$12,800,000
24%	3	$51,200,000

"Forget about 18 percent—let's go for 24 percent," said Cindy. "That way, we will have over $50 million dollars by the time Scott and I are ready to retire. I think I'm finally starting to enjoy all this financial stuff."

"I don't mean to burst your bubble, Cindy, but 24 percent is all but impossible," I said. "You hear in the news about stocks like Dell and Qualcomm that have gone up hundreds of percents, but those are the exception and not the rule. And keep in mind, when stocks go sky-high like that, it increases the possibility of a crash. And I'm not just talking about the Great Depression or Black Monday in 1987. In March of 2000, technology stocks went down more than 30 percent in less than a month."

I knew Darius would spend more time on this, but I wanted to plant a seed that there are many risks associated with investing. Since Black Monday in October of 1987, a day when the stock market tumbled dramatically, stocks have performed incredibly well. Because of that, it's very easy to have unrealistic expectations about the market.

Dr. Lori continued: "It is not worth harming your mental health to take on all that risk. I have dealt with too many patients who have incredible stress from losses in the stock market. Aside from feeling comfortable psychologically before you can make your first investment, you must follow some basic rules."

I was hoping that Cindy and Scott weren't getting too caught up in the "get-rich-quick" environment of New York. As the skyscrapers on Wall Street came into view, I knew that the thought of getting rich and earning big returns was running through their minds. The purpose of investing is to grow assets and keep up with inflation. Using investing as a means of getting rich quickly is why so many day traders and market speculators go broke.

Dr. Lori handed Cindy a note with her three simple rules and said, "Before you invest, make sure you have done the following."

Dr. Lori's Rules Before You Invest

1. You must be running a surplus in your Vital Signs.
2. You need three months of living expenses in cash.
3. You cannot have any debt with an interest rate above 10 percent.

Before Cindy and Scott could get discouraged, I quickly interjected. "Keep in mind, you have $25,000 in your 401(k) account and you need to understand how to invest it. Just because you don't meet the conditions of these rules now, it doesn't mean that you won't in the future."

Dr. Lori was already one step ahead of me. "I want to show you an example of how you can get started with investing, in addition to your 401(k) savings. Remember that the greatest factor in accumulating wealth is time. The power of compound interest is incredible, and there is a technique called dollar cost averaging that is a great way for you to get started. Dollar cost averaging simply means that you put a set dollar amount into an investment every month. It's a way to invest in the stock market that allows you protection against the market's ups and downs."

I was glad that Dr. Lori and I had worked on this example, but before we showed Cindy and Scott the chart, it was critical that we went over some important points. The first was inflation. Many times, investment professionals show the impact of investing but don't bother factoring inflation into their results. What students really want to know is *not* how much their money will be worth in the future, but what they can actually buy with that money in the future. A buck and a quarter could buy you a steak dinner for two during the Depression, but today it's lucky to get you a side order of steak fries. And as long as inflation continues along at its current pace of about 2 percent a year, money will be worth substantially less in the future than it is worth today—which means it will buy considerably less. It sounds ridiculous to think that you'll be paying twelve bucks for a cappuccino in seventy years, but the numbers bear it out.

I tried to bring this point home to Cindy and Scott and said, "If you earn 12 percent on an investment, you are really earning only about 10 percent, because inflation is 2 percent a year. Think about it like this: If your money is wrapped in tinfoil in your freezer, it will be worth a lot less by the time you let it thaw out. You must remember that you invest not only to grow your money but also to offset inflation."

Cindy and Scott nodded, and I had to add one more important point before we got to the chart. Just as the government gives a financial incentive to home buyers by allowing them to deduct mortgage payments from their taxes, it also provides many tax incentives to save money. The government knows that those who save their own money put less of a strain on society. As a result, Uncle Sam provides a tax break for those who are willing to save.

Seemingly reading my mind, Dr. Lori elaborated. "The benefit of accounts such as your 401(k) or an individual retirement account, often called an IRA, is that your money grows tax-free. By taking advantage of tax-deferred accounts, you save a fortune in taxes and your money grows incredibly faster."

Many investors don't understand that when you open up a normal brokerage account—or make any investment, for that matter—the realized profits are taxed. There is constant debate about whether this is fair, but the fact remains that the only way to combat these taxes on investments, called capital gains taxes, is to use tax-deferred accounts such as a 401(k) or an IRA. It was okay if Cindy and Scott didn't quite understand this yet, since I knew Darius would be covering it in more detail.

At this point, we were finally ready to show the dollar cost averaging chart. The assumptions we made were as follows:

1. The starting balance in the account is zero.
2. The investment will be made monthly. Fifty-dollar and $100 investments are in the table.
3. The average rate of return will be 12 percent.
4. Inflation will be 2 percent.
5. The money will go into an IRA, which is tax-deferred.

Dollar Cost Averaging into a Tax-Deferred Account

Number of years	Investing $50/month	Investing $100/month
10	$10,128	$20,256
20	$37,017	$74,034
30	$108,405	$216,809
40	$297,932	$595,864
50	$801,109	$1,602,217

"Those numbers are mind-boggling," said Cindy. "You are right about the power of compound interest!"

Cindy had every right to be enthused. This chart brought to light exactly what Dr. Lori said right when we got in the car. *The most significant factor in investing is how long you invest your money.* The reason is that the longer your money is invested, the more time it has to double. Pretend for a second you're playing golf with a friend and you bet one dollar on the first hole. If you then double your bet every hole, by the time you get to the ninth hole, the bet would be up to $256. On the eighteenth hole, because of the power of compounding, the bet would be up to $131,072! You better hit a good tee shot.

We were just outside Darius's office, but Dr. Lori wasn't quite finished. "If you could just discipline yourself to have that money automatically taken from your checking account each month, you probably wouldn't even miss it," she said. "It's called *paying yourself first.*"

It was a great point—pay yourself first—yet it's something that so few of us do. We always find a way to get the rent and the car payment taken care of, but it seems like the bank account is empty when it comes time to invest. That's why those in the know—think Katie—pay themselves first by having a set amount automatically withdrawn from their paycheck or checking account and invested into an IRA.

When Scott said, "I still think it's a little ridiculous to list the returns for fifty years," I said to him, "Go tell that to someone who is eighteen years old—or eight years old, for that matter. If nothing else, this chart should show you that the best time to start saving for a kid's education is *before* that kid is born!"

Dr. Lori pulled over when she got to Darius's office building, and I was thrilled with all the information we had covered. I'm a lucky guy to have such smart friends. We all thanked Dr. Lori and set our sights on the hallowed halls of Wall Street. With Darius looming, I knew we would have our work cut out for us.

Exercise 7

A. Create your balance sheet. List liabilities from highest to lowest interest rate.

Assets		**Liabilities**	
Cash/Checking		Credit cards	
Savings		Credit union	
Car 1		Car 1	
Car 2		Car 2	
Stocks, bonds, etc.		Student loans	
Retirement plans		Personal loan	
Total Assets		**Total Liabilities**	
		Owner's Equity	

Total Assets: ______
Total Liabilities: ______
______
Owner's Equity: ______
(Net worth)

B. For all your investments, including your 401(k), IRA, and any other pension or brokerage accounts, find out what you are investing in. The best place to start is the benefits department of your company.

Example:
401(k) fund: 25% Aggressive Growth, 50% Growth and Income, 25% Bonds, or:

50 shares of Microsoft
30 shares of Home Depot
20 shares of Coca-Cola

Chapter 8

Understand the Risks and Rewards of Investing

The fastest way to double your money is to fold it over and put it in your pocket.

—Texas Bix Binder

My mom taught me my first lesson in investing when I was seven years old. One day, I was being my usual persistent self and kept saying, "Mom, can I have a Coke? Mom, can I have a Coke? Mom, can I have a Coke? Mom, can I have a Coke? Mom, can I have a Coke? Mom, can I have a Coke?" in rapid-fire succession. I guess I was pretty thirsty.

As always, my mom had an answer. She decided to put a piece of masking tape on seven Cokes with my name written in black Magic Marker on each one. She then said, "Here are your Cokes for the next week. You can have all of them now if you want or you can have one a day. Just remember, I'm not going to the store again until next Sunday."

I drank four and a half Cokes that night and the caffeine kept me up half the night. I drank what was left that afternoon, and by Tuesday night, I was begging again. "Mom, I'll go to the supermarket with you and help you carry the Cokes." She didn't fall for the chivalry, and sure enough, the lesson was learned. My mom calls it the "Candy Lesson," named after one of my favorites as a kid, Now 'N Laters, whose slogan was "Have one for now and save one for later." What I learned from the experience is that a key to balancing financial success and happiness is finding the right mix of living for the moment and saving for the future.

I was thinking about this as we walked toward Darius's highbrow office overlooking lower Manhattan. Everything was plush, and Cindy and Scott seemed impressed—and maybe a little intimidated—by their surroundings. This kind of office is the norm for people like Darius—a professional money manager who is paid big bucks to invest for individuals worth hundreds of millions of dollars.

As was his custom, Darius started by getting Cindy and Scott involved and asked, "Who is the best person in the world you can invest in?"

"Warren Buffett," said Cindy. "He's that investor who's made a zillion dollars, right?"

"Wrong!" exclaimed Darius. "Well, you're right about who Warren Buffett is, but you're wrong about who the best person in the world you can invest in is. The answer to that question is *you*! You are the best person in the world you can invest in. If there's one thing you take away from this little meeting, it's to *invest in yourself*."

Darius went on to explain how he had advised his younger brother to take a bartending course for $150 and how the investment had already paid off tens of thousands of dollars. As a teacher making $23,000 a year, Darius's brother would not have been able to keep his Vital Signs positive without the additional income he made by tending bar on the weekends. The course he took was much more valuable than any stock he could buy. Darius continued, "Markets are very uncertain creatures, and trying to make your money based on something so uncertain is very risky. By investing in yourself, you have the ability to control the return on your investment."

"My company gives an extra $5,000 a year to any employee who learns a foreign language," said Cindy. "Is that what you mean?"

"That's a great example," said Darius. "Another one is spending

$600 to take a seminar in Web design and then starting a small business where you charge $25 an hour to design other people's Web sites. After three days of work, you'll have paid for the course."

Because Darius understood the risks and complexities of financial markets, he always gave my students the same advice: to invest in themselves. He also could tell that Cindy and Scott were itching to learn the basics of the markets, and for this we were well prepared.

Plan of Attack

Before I came to New York with Cindy and Scott, Darius and I had spent quite a bit of time planning for this session. We knew that we could talk for months about this subject, and we wanted to make sure we covered everything and still not overwhelm Cindy and Scott, who were novices on the subject of investing. We drew up an outline, and because Darius has a tendency to be very detailed, we decided that he would do most of the explaining and I would keep us on the task at hand. Now that we were all together in Darius's office, we showed our outline to Cindy and Scott.

1. Three Primary Types of Investments
   a. Explain stocks, bonds, and cash
   b. Incorporate into the Rule of 72
2. Definitions
   a. Define what the stock market is: Dow Jones, S&P 500, NASDAQ 100
   b. Bull and Bear market—bullish or bearish?
   c. Explain what a mutual fund is and how it works
   d. Describe the types of tax-deferred accounts, such as 401(k), IRA, and Roth IRA
3. Darius's Hierarchy of Investing—Nine Rules for Investing, including:
   a. Risk tolerance and time horizon

   b. How to minimize fees and taxes
   c. Asset allocation and choosing investments
4. Choosing an Investment Firm
   a. How to find the right place to invest
   b. The importance of the Internet

Three Primary Types of Investments

Darius began as planned: "I want to give you an overview of investing. I know Dr. Lori showed you the Rule of 72, but she didn't talk about *how* you can earn those types of returns. Can you think of some things that you can invest in?"

"How about stamps or coins or real estate, art, or even a savings account, stocks, or mutual funds. I can think of hundreds of things," said Scott.

"That's a great list," said Darius, "and if you really think about it, it's possible to invest in almost anything. Just to keep it simple, today we are going to focus on the three primary types of investments: equity, debt, and cash. People typically refer to equity as stocks and to debt as bonds."

"Wait a second, Darius," Scott said. "Why is a stock called equity?"

Darius loved to teach, and his adrenaline started pumping the minute he realized that Cindy and Scott were so interested. "Suppose you buy stock in IBM," he said. "What you are doing is buying a part of the company. Therefore, you are an owner, which is also called a shareholder, of the company. That means that you own equity in the company."

"Why would I want to be an owner of a company?" asked Cindy.

"Because as an owner, your stake in the company increases in value as the company increases in value, and you actually make money in one of two ways," said Darius. "When the company has extra profits that they don't need to plow back into the business, the shareholders receive a check, which is known as a dividend. The other way you make money is when the value of your company's stock increases. If you paid $100 for a share of stock, and a few months later the stock is selling for $110, you have gained 10 percent on your initial stock investment."

"When would we actually see that money?" asked Cindy, who was asking all the right questions.

"Dividends typically get paid every three months," said Darius. "You see the money from the appreciation of the stock only when you sell your shares, thus giving up your stake in the company."

"So when I hold on to a stock, my only gains are on paper?" asked Scott.

He was absolutely right. Many students think that the way to get rich is to trade, but every time you sell an investment that has gone up, you are hit with a tax bill—unless it is in a tax-deferred account such as a 401(k) or an IRA. Darius responded to Scott, "If a stock goes up but you continue to hold it, you don't have to pay any taxes—that's why you typically want to buy and *hold,* not buy and *sell,* stocks."

It was time to address debt, and I was anxious for Cindy and Scott to view debt from the perspective of a corporation. There are two primary differences between debt for corporations and debt for individuals. The first is that debt costs a lot less for corporations since they typically pay a much lower interest rate than individuals and they also get a significant tax break. The other, more subtle difference is that corporations take on debt for investments, not expenses. Paying 20 percent interest so you can get the kids the latest Pokémon toy and paying 8 percent interest to build a new research lab for new product development are two totally different animals.

Reading my thoughts, Darius started talking about debt: "Another way for a company to raise money is to sell debt in the form of a bond. Suppose IBM needs to raise some money to build a new factory and doesn't want to sell equity to do so. Instead of selling ownership of the company by selling stock, the company will borrow the money by selling debt. For example, you give them $1,000 and they give you a piece of paper called a bond. The bond will specify the interest rate and the term of the loan. In this case, the loan might last for one year and pay you 7 percent interest."

"So it's guaranteed?" Cindy asked, showing that she was keen on an essential element of investing: *determining risk.*

Darius took the question head-on: "As long as IBM is in good financial shape, they will certainly make good on the bond. Solid companies, often called blue chips, almost never default on their bonds, but they also don't pay you a very high interest rate. Riskier companies, like that new dot-com your brother keeps nagging you about, pay very high rates of interest, maybe as high as 14 percent, but also carry enormous risk considering they're a good bet to default. Bonds like these are known as junk bonds. The opposite of junk bonds are government bonds, which are backed by the United States government and offer returns of about 6 percent with very little risk."

I nodded at Darius, who quickly shifted to talking about cash before being interrupted by Scott, who suddenly had a big grin on his face. "How can you call cash an investment when it just sits there and gets eaten up by inflation?" he asked, showing how proud he was of himself for picking up this tip from Dr. Lori's lesson. I was indeed impressed, and knew, no doubt, that Darius had the right answer.

"Cash refers to a very liquid investment such as a checking account, a certificate of deposit—better known as a CD—or a money market fund," said Darius. "It's called cash because you typically can turn the investment into cash very quickly and it has very low risk."

"Low risk and you can turn it into cash right away, sounds like the way to go," said Scott.

I knew that we had been talking a lot about risk and reward, but we hadn't specifically addressed this concept. Risk and reward describes the relationship between how much an investment will go up and its level of risk. A high-risk investment might be a trendy bar and grill that has only a 10 percent chance of making it big, but if it does make it big, it will triple your investment. A low-risk investment is earning 2 percent in a savings account at a major bank.

Darius brought this to light: "If it has low risk, it also probably has a low rate of return. Earning only 5 percent is not going to be enough to finance your future. There are no free lunches in investing, and it's vital that you find investments with the best risk-and-reward ratio."

At this point, Darius had presented the three primary types of investments, and I wanted to do a quick review. "Before we talk about how all this affects the Rule of 72, can you two just remind me of the three types of investments?" I asked.

"There's stocks, also called equities," Cindy called out. "There's bonds, also called debt. And then there's cash."

"You got it, Cindy," and we all looked at the chart that Darius prepared.

Investment	Also Called	Typical Return	Level of Risk
Equity	Stocks	12%	Medium to high
Debt	Bonds	7%	Low to medium
Cash	Money markets, CDs	5%	Almost none

Before Darius started to explain the chart, he said, "You will notice that I use the word *typical* a lot in this section, since there are very few absolutes when it comes to investments. For example, the stock market was up 37.5 percent in 1995 but was up only 1.26 percent in 1994. There are some years that your investments will lose money, even in the blue-chip stocks. In the bear market of 1973 to 1974, Coca-Cola decreased by 70 percent, General Motors 66 percent, and Walt Disney 85 percent. On the other hand, an investment of $10,000 in Yahoo! in 1997 would be worth over a million dollars in the year 2000. For stocks, the typical return is 12 percent, but it fluctuates by huge margins—not only year to year, but day to day."

Darius had done a great job of explaining the chart, but it apparently struck a chord with Cindy, who said, "I feel like Dr. Lori created a little bit of false hope for us. She got me all excited about the Rule of 72, and I started thinking that we were going to have

$50 million to retire on. Now that I understand the relationship between risk and return, I see how unrealistic that is."

It is unrealistic, I thought, but there are a lot of people out there hocking investments that offer extremely high rates of return, and it can be very enticing for my students to want to buy into one of these. There was even a Gallup poll cited in *Barron's* on February 21, 2000, that over the next decade, investors thought the stock market would return a gain of 19 percent a year. Talk about unrealistic expectations! What Darius did was show them that while high returns are possible, they always carry higher risk. If Cindy hadn't already learned this from her brother Brent, I knew it would only be a matter of time before she did.

While Darius had been talking, I wrote down how the different rates of return impact the Rule of 72. I handed it to Darius, who said, "Look at the disparity in the growth of $25,000 when you look at rates of return of 6 percent, 8 percent, and 12 percent."

Annual Rate of Return	Years to Double Money	Value of $25,000 in 36 Years
6%	12	$200,000
8%	9	$400,000
12%	6	$1,600,000

"I know it may seem like I'm waffling on this," Darius explained, "but I want to drill into your heads that it's critical to maximize your rate of return without taking on unnecessary risk. You are going to have a difficult time financing your retirement if you earn a return of only 6 percent. If you can earn 12 percent—and by investing in stocks you can—you are looking at a very nice nest egg."

I thought about students of mine who wanted to leave their money in a savings account, or even worse, in an old coffee jar, until I showed them this same little chart. I also have had students who have gone broke by investing in risky ventures that promised to return 35 percent. But when all is said and done, the stock market is usually the best place for long-term growth.

Definitions

When it comes to investing, one of the most common questions I get is "What the heck is the stock market?" It was no accident that Darius started with this definition. "When people talk about the stock market, they are often talking about different things," he said. "The reason we talk about the stock market as a whole is that we want some frame of reference to measure how stocks are doing. When we talk about the Dow Jones Industrial Average, it refers to the stocks of thirty big, blue-chip companies such as Wal-Mart, Coca-Cola, Home Depot, General Electric, and General Motors. There is a formula that comes up with the value of all thirty stocks combined and that produces the Dow Jones Industrial Average. Right now, the Dow Jones is at about 11,000."

"And what does that tell us?" asked Scott.

"Nothing really," said Darius. "It's just a measure of those thirty stocks, but if you asked me what the market did today and I told you the Dow Jones was up 110 points, you would know that those thirty stocks, on average, went up about 1 percent. The media, and not so much investment professionals, will track the performance of this index as an illustration of how stocks 'in general' are performing."

"Okay, but if there are thousands of stocks, knowing what thirty stocks did on any given day doesn't really tell me that much," said Cindy, just as we thought she would.

"Which is why there is another index, called the S&P [Standard and Poor's] 500, which measures five hundred of the biggest stocks and includes companies like Ford, The Gap, and Campbell Soup," I answered. "Investment professionals use this 'index' because it gives a better picture of how the overall market is doing. Five hundred stocks paints a better picture than thirty stocks."

"I agree," said Darius, "so from here on out, when I refer to the stock market, I mean the S&P 500. And the historical average return of the S&P 500 is about 12 percent."

The other index that I knew we needed to mention was the

NASDAQ 100. The NASDAQ is actually a separate marketplace from the New York Stock Exchange, but the details weren't relevant to Cindy and Scott. Darius explained: "The NASDAQ 100 is an index of the one hundred biggest companies on the exchange and is made up primarily of technology giants such as Microsoft, Dell, Cisco, Oracle, and Intel. It measures the performance of technology companies, which means it tends to offer more growth but with more risk than the Dow Jones and the S&P 500."

I was thankful that we covered all these indices, since knowing what it means to talk about the "stock market" was a critical first step. The words "bull" and "bear" are common on Wall Street and are used to describe the direction of the stock market. Darius explained, "When people talk about a bull market, they mean that the stock market is increasing in value. If you hear an analyst say that she's bullish on the S&P 500, it means that she thinks the index is going up. If she's bearish, then she thinks the market is going down. If you ever forget, just remember that a bull's horns always point upward—hence the upward trend of a bullish market."

Since the fall of 1987, U.S. stocks have experienced a bull market—an unprecedented period of thirteen years in which stock prices have been on the rise. Within that period of time, there have been plenty of weeks and months in which the stock market has decreased, but the overall trend has been bullish. It's important for investors not to forget that occasional bear markets are the norm, not the exception, and the only way to protect against them is a commitment to long-term investing.

It was now time to talk about mutual funds, and Darius took control: "A mutual fund is nothing more than a pool of money managed by a professional money manager. Many people don't understand what they are because there are so many different kinds. Some mutual funds invest only in stocks, others only in bonds, some in foreign stocks, some in stocks and bonds, and some only in big companies. The list is endless, but just remember that a mutual fund is a pool of investments managed by professionals who charge a fee."

"How many stocks can a mutual fund invest in?" asked Scott.

"Some mutual funds own several hundred stocks," said Darius, "and the main reason is diversification. Putting all your eggs in one basket is risky, which is why it's so important to diversify. Most individual investors understand this concept, but at the same time, they don't want to go out and buy a bunch of stocks. For one, the commissions are expensive when you do that, and second, most investors wouldn't know what to buy."

"Okay, so you give your money to this mutual fund and some professional does all the work," said Cindy. "They do the research, pick the stocks, and make sure you are diversified. But how do they get paid, and do most of them earn that pay?"

"They get paid two ways," explained Darius. "The first is an up-front sales charge, which is called a load. Fidelity Magellan, for example, one of the biggest mutual funds in the world, will charge you 3 percent up front for the privilege of owning its fund. So if you want to invest $2,000, $60 goes to pay for the load. There's also an expense called a management fee. The fund will take expenses of .6 percent out of your investment each year to pay for the expenses of running the fund. Some funds take out as much as 3 percent a year, and the average is about 1.5 percent."

"One point five percent sounds pretty reasonable, especially if they are professionals who study the market and make good decisions," said Scott.

I was thankful for the great dialogue and was pleased to let Darius explain. "Let's back up a second—not all mutual funds charge an up-front fee. In fact, I would advise you not to buy a fund that charges a load, since there is no evidence that funds with a load outperform no-load funds."

"So why would anyone pay a load?" asked Cindy.

"Because that person needs service or assistance in choosing a fund," said Darius. "Loads are for people who do not want to do any research and would prefer to let a broker make decisions for them. If you are the one who takes the time to select a mutual fund, then by no means should you pay a load. However, if you are not comfortable doing the research and want personalized service, there are good brokers out there who will do the research for you and charge you accordingly."

I was glad Darius presented it this way. Using a full-service broker—or full-service anything, for that matter—is expensive, but the true professionals earn their fee. I actually have two accounts: One is with a full-service broker who helps me make decisions and who, in his words, "helps protect me from myself." The other account is with a limited-service brokerage firm that offers hundreds of no-load mutual funds and charges me only between $15 and $25 if I want to buy or sell a stock.

Darius got us back on track and said, "I want to address that second fee, the management fee, which is called the 'expense ratio.' The expense ratio for mutual funds can be as high as 2 percent or 3 percent. So if you had $20,000 in a mutual fund that charged a 2 percent expense fee, the fund would take out $400 a year to cover expenses every year."

"Over thirty years, that's more than ten grand," said Scott.

"Twelve grand, to be exact," said Darius, "not to mention that the money they took out would have grown even more. But there are funds that charge much less. In fact, some funds charge as low as .2 percent. So on that same $20,000, they take out $40 instead of $400. It's like the difference between paying a bookie $2 or $20 to place a thousand-dollar bet. I don't know about you, but I've never heard of any poor bookies—or mutual fund managers, for that matter."

I knew Darius was providing the necessary background to talk about index funds, my favorite type of investment. He continued, "Remember we talked about the S&P 500—the index of the 500 biggest stocks? Mutual fund managers use the return of that index to measure their performance. Because everyone knows that the stock market fluctuates, comparing returns against the S&P 500 index is a way for mutual fund managers to gauge their specific performance against the overall stock market. Are you with me?"

"I think what you're saying," said Cindy, "is that the S&P 500 is like the barometer for the stock market, and you can use it to compare the returns of mutual funds to see how they are performing relative to the overall market."

"You got it," said Darius. "You'll hear mutual fund managers brag in their advertisements about how they outperformed the S&P 500 by 10 percent or 20 percent or whatever."

"That's the fund I want to buy—the one that beats the market," said Scott. "If I'm paying a professional money manager a fee, I would expect nothing less."

"You and every other investor," I said, "but the problem is that most mutual funds *don't* beat the index. According to Lipper Analytical Services, 80 percent of all mutual funds have failed to beat the S&P 500 over the last three years ending December 31, 1999. I also saw on the Motley Fool Web site that during the 1990s, the S&P 500 outperformed the average diversified mutual fund by approximately 3.4 percent per year. In other words, if you invested $10,000 with one of those high-paid investment managers—no offense, Darius—it would have been worth $36,748. On the other hand, if you invested $10,000 in the S&P 500, it would have been worth $49,315."

"If the mutual fund managers are so smart and so well paid, then why are they getting whipped by the S&P 500 index?" asked Scott.

Darius, a professional money manager himself, said, "For one, because they are charging fees, which means they are playing catch-up to make up for all their expenses—like this fancy office and my high-powered computer. And two, beating the stock market is one of the toughest things in the world to do—tougher than hitting a baseball traveling at 100 miles per hour. But without going into all the details of why, let's just say that the market is so complex that we're not even going to try to beat it."

"So what are we going to do, lose to it?" asked Cindy. "I thought we wanted to make some money in the market."

Our goal, as Darius was to explain, was to match the market by earning the same returns as the S&P 500. Because so many investors have the appetite to do the same, mutual funds called "index" funds have been created to give investors the same return as a particular index. There are index funds for, among others, the Dow Jones, the NASDAQ 100, and, most prominently, the S&P 500. These funds provide the benefit of diversification at a very low cost, and that's why I invest in them myself.

Darius elaborated: "There are mutual funds out there that strictly buy and sell the stocks that make up the S&P 500. Because they don't have to pay managers to do research, they typically do not charge a load and they charge very low expenses, as low as eighteen cents per one hundred dollars. I know this because after years of investing, this is where I choose to put most of my own money. That way, I don't have to worry about the day-to-day fluctuations in the market. I know that, for a very small fee, I am going to earn the same return as the S&P 500, which, historically, grows at a rate of about 12 percent. I never win and I never lose when I compare my return to the overall market."

Tax-Deferred Accounts—401(k), IRA, Roth IRA

Darius moved us along to the different types of tax-deferred accounts. Dr. Lori had already touched on the benefits of tax-deferred investing in her dollar cost averaging example, but I felt it was important to review.

Believe it or not, the government actually wants you to save money, and because of that, it has created some tax breaks to encourage you to do so. I wanted to start by defining a 401(k) plan. By the way, if you are in the not-for-profit sector, a 401(k) is similar to a 403B/TSA plan and the definitions are essentially interchangeable. A 457 plan is a nonqualified deferred compensation plan for states, counties, cities, and agencies and has some similarities to a 401(k). Darius pulled up the definition of a 401(k) on his computer and asked Cindy to read it aloud.

> A 401(k) plan is a retirement savings plan that is funded by employee contributions and often matching contributions from the employer. The major attraction of these plans is that the contributions are taken from pretax salary, and the funds grow tax-free until withdrawn. Also, the plans are to some extent self-directed, and they are portable . . .

There was a bunch of fine print, but those were the essentials. Darius got right to a practical example: "Suppose your salary is $30,000 and your tax rate is 25 percent. Don't be intimidated by the numbers—just follow along. Ordinarily, you would pay 25 percent of your $30,000 salary in taxes, which is $7,500. But if you put 10 percent of your salary, which is $3,000, into a 401(k), you now only pay taxes based on income of $27,000. Stay with me here—25 percent of $27,000 is $6,750. So, in other words, the government is forgiving you of $750 in taxes so that you can invest for your retirement—not a bad deal, when you think about it."

Another advantage of a 401(k) is that many companies provide additional funding to an employee's 401(k)—often called the company match. It's a way for companies to show employees that they are committed to their future. To an employee, it's a great perk because the amount that the company invests in the 401(k) doesn't count as income and it grows tax free. It is a great benefit that employees really need to look at closely when evaluating their compensation.

As I was thinking this, Cindy asked, "And before I forget, what does portable and self-directed mean?"

"*Portable* means that if you leave your job, you can transfer the account to your next employer's 401(k) or to your own brokerage account. This stuff can get complicated, and I recommend going to the benefits department of your company to ask questions—that's what they are there for. As for the term *self-directed,* it means you get to choose the investments within your 401(k)."

I knew this was important to address. Many of my students complain that their companies provide no direction when it comes time to select the investments in their 401(k). Most new employees just get a blank form with a bunch of mutual funds and have no idea what to do. I tell my students under the age of fifty that they should invest in stocks, preferably an S&P 500 index fund.

Darius continued: "I just showed you how you save money in taxes when you put your money into a 401(k), but what I didn't mention is that once the money goes into the account, it grows without having to pay taxes."

This point was so important that I wanted to make sure they understood. "If you invest in a non-tax-deferred account—let's say you just call a broker and buy a stock—if that stock goes up and you sell it, you get hit with a capital gains tax bill. However, if you have your money in a 401(k) and you buy and sell the same stock, you don't pay any taxes. It makes a huge difference."

Darius continued with the definitions. "Other tax-free accounts include an IRA, Roth IRA, Sep-IRA, and Keogh. Sep-IRA and Keogh plans are for the self-employed and follow the same principles as the 401(k). As you may already know, an IRA stands for individual retirement account, and you can contribute up to $2,000 per year *each* as long as your joint income is below $160,000. If you contribute a total of $4,000 to an IRA, you immediately receive a tax benefit, just like that of a 401(k). If your tax rate is 25 percent, you would effectively get $1,000 of your investment back in the form of a lower tax bill."

Darius was rolling, and I knew he was going to address the difference between a traditional and a Roth IRA—a topic that students always wanted clarity on. "The Roth IRA is different from a regular IRA in two ways," he said. "First, you don't get a tax break when you put money into a Roth IRA. Unlike the IRA, which will save you $1,000 in taxes when you contribute $4,000, the Roth IRA offers no such tax refund."

This is not a subtle difference. The great thing about an IRA—and a 401(k), for that matter—is that it puts money right back into your pocket when you save for your future. It's the ultimate rebate. With a Roth IRA, there is no tax advantage when you make the investment, but once the money is invested in a Roth IRA, it does grow tax-free just like an IRA. Darius explained why a Roth IRA was still viewed by some as a better investment than a traditional IRA. "The biggest difference is that when you take the money out of a Roth IRA at retirement, you don't have to pay *any* taxes at all. The bad part about your traditional IRA is that even though you get a refund when you invest and the money grows tax-deferred, you have to pay taxes when you withdraw the money upon retirement."

Scott was obviously following, because he made the perfect analogy: "So with the traditional IRA, you get a break on the way in and pay taxes on the way out. With a Roth IRA, you don't get a break on the way in, but you get a free ride on the way out. So which one do you think we should get?"

"There is actually quite a bit of disagreement in the investment world about which is better, but it's a judgment call," said Darius. "If you don't have any credit card debt, I would go with the Roth, but if you have high-interest debt, I would go for the traditional and use your tax rebate to pay off that debt."

At this point, we had covered the first two sections of our outline and the tough part was behind us. Darius asked for a few minutes to check on the markets, which I took as an opportunity to introduce Cindy and Scott to the street vendors of New York. The hot dogs and the knishes did not disappoint, and with full bellies, we were ready for Darius's hierarchy.

Darius's Hierarchy—9 Rules for Successful Investing

Darius seemed pleased that the market was up, and after pointing out that I spilled some mustard on my brand-new white lab coat, he handed each of us a copy of his hierarchy and began, "There are nine rules about investing, and by now you should understand most of them."

Darius's Hierarchy—9 Rules for Successful Investing

1. Above all, invest in yourself.
2. Your Vital Signs must be showing a surplus.
3. You must have three months of living expenses in cash.
4. You cannot have any debt with an interest rate above 10 percent.
5. Determine time horizon and risk tolerance.
6. Minimize fees.
7. Minimize taxes—accept the gift from Uncle Sam.
8. Determine asset allocation.
9. Track the performance of your investments.

After studying the list, I quickly realized that we had already explained rules one through four very thoroughly. Investing in yourself had been explained by Darius, and rules two through four were the same as Dr. Lori's "Rules Before You Invest."

Darius saw this, too, and quickly summed it up: "After you have exhausted all productive ways to invest in yourself, your Vital Signs must be in positive territory, and you need to have enough cash to pay all of your living expenses for three months. The last thing you want to do is go in debt on your credit card or have to sell an investment to meet your monthly expenses. And remember, by paying off debt, you are making a risk-free investment."

"It wouldn't make sense to buy a stock and then have to sell it to buy groceries," said Cindy.

"Which leads me to rule five," Darius said. "The sooner you think you will need the money, the less risk you should take on. If you are putting away money for a vacation in six months or a down payment on a house in a year, you don't want to buy stocks. Over a short period of time, stocks can decline dramatically. By the same token, given your age, you want a high return in your retirement account and don't need to worry about short-term fluctuations, so stocks are probably the way to go."

"Why do you say probably?" Cindy asked.

"Because of the second part of rule five—determining risk tolerance," he said. "If it's going to make your stomach queasy to see your investments go up and down in value, you really should not own stocks. Sometimes you need to throw out the numbers and think about your comfort level."

"That's exactly what Dr. Lori said," said Cindy. "You're making it sound like stocks are really risky."

"Long-term stocks have proven to be a good investment, but there have been times when stock prices have plummeted. They are called 'crashes,' and they often lead to panic. In your mind, you just have to be mentally prepared for the fact that the stock market could go down by 10 percent or more on any given day. In 1973, the S&P 500 was down 17 percent, and in 1974, it was down another 30 percent. And even more recently, in October of 1997, the S&P 500 decreased by 11 percent."

"Why are you trying to scare us so much, Darius?" asked Scott.

"I'm just giving you the facts. From 1995 to 1999, the stock market increased by an average of over 28 percent per year, and the public has been starting to think that the stock market goes only one way—up and up and up. I don't want you to start thinking that 28 percent returns are a given, much less the norm. And I also want you to be aware that stocks, like any investment, can go down. It all comes back to risk and reward."

Continuing, Darius explained, "Rule number six is to minimize fees. Keep in mind, there is almost always a fee involved when you buy an investment, but the key is to keep that fee as low as possible. For example, the fee to buy one hundred shares of IBM could be as low as $8 or as high as $300, depending on whom you buy it from."

"Why would anyone pay $300?" asked Scott.

"Because not only are they paying for the stock, but they are also paying for advice and service. Brokers who charge high commissions can justify their fees because of the personalized service that they offer. When you pay a low fee, it's because you are only paying to execute your trade, not for any service and guidance."

The best way to minimize fees and match the market returns is by buying index funds. Vanguard was the pioneer in these funds, and most of the major investment firms have since caught on and offer index funds. Once again, I think the best way to invest is to put aside an amount into an S&P 500 index fund by using dollar cost averaging.

Darius got us back on track: "We're going to address choosing an investment firm in detail, but for now, let's move on to rule number seven, minimizing taxes—an investor's number-one enemy. We have already discussed the importance of using tax-deferred accounts, but I also want to talk about the tax advantages of buying and holding versus trading. In a normal brokerage account, meaning a non-tax-deferred account, every time you sell a stock that has appreciated, you are subject to commissions and capital gains taxes."

Before Darius continued, I wanted to explain what he meant by a "normal" brokerage account: "As investors, you want to 'max out' the contributions to your tax-deferred accounts, such as your 401(k) and IRA. However, once those accounts are maxed out, you still want to invest, even though the money doesn't grow tax-deferred. One way to avoid paying taxes is to buy and hold. Remember, even when your money is not in a tax-deferred account, you don't have to pay taxes unless there is a realized gain. Your net worth will be higher, but because your gains are only on paper, you don't pay taxes until you sell the investment. In other words, *buying and holding is tax-free investing.*"

"Just so I'm hearing you right," said Scott. "What you're saying is that, even in a normal brokerage account, I will not have to pay taxes as long as I hold my investments?"

This was a great question, but it was also a tad tricky. We had mentioned before about the two ways to profit from owning a stock—either by receiving a dividend or by the stock appreciating. Dividend checks are subject to taxes, so there is often a tax bill even when you buy and hold. For most stocks, dividends are small and relatively insignificant. Darius explained, "Not all stocks pay a dividend, and most that do, pay a rather small one at that. You still don't have to pay taxes on the appreciation of the investment, however, until you actually sell it."

"So if we open up a 'normal' brokerage account and buy eBay for $50 a share and it goes to $500 a share, we don't have to pay a cent in taxes as long as we hold on to it?" asked Cindy.

Cindy was indeed correct, and Scott followed this up with another question: "So why are people always trading? To tell you the truth, I always thought that was the way to get rich."

This question seemed to fire Darius up as he said, "First of all, people who trade either don't understand the tax implications or think that they know so much about the market that they can still beat it, even after paying the taxes. Remember what I said—most professionals can't even beat the market. Think about it: When you try to trade stocks to beat the market, you have to pay commissions every time you trade, as well as taxes every time you make money on an investment. That's a lot of catching up to do, and it's an impossible climb for most investors. It's similar to the 'take-out' at a racetrack. Even if you win your bet, you don't get a full return on your investment because the track usually withholds between 10 percent and 25 percent of the pool for providing the 'service' of taking your bet. Casinos are no different. Most payouts in a casino are given after the casino has taken its cut. It's called the vigorish, and it's why the racetracks, casinos, and investment firms always make money—at your expense.

"The bottom line: Minimize fees, use tax-free investments, and buy and hold your stocks," said Darius. "Now let's move on to rule number eight: Determine asset allocation. You now know that there are three types of investments—equity, debt, and cash. You also know their typical returns and their level of risk. Now all you have to do is figure out what percentage of each you should have."

"I wouldn't know where to start," said Cindy.

This was another question we anticipated, and Darius was ready with a reply: "The first thing to remember is that the longer the time horizon, the more risk you should be willing to take.

Money for retirement should be invested in stocks, because there is plenty of time to ride out short-term fluctuations. But I wouldn't necessarily tell your parents the same thing. The closer you are to needing the money, the more conservative of an investment you should use. Let's try a quick quiz to see if we're on the same page. I'm going to give you a piece of paper with some things that you might need money for, and you tell me which type of investment is the best."

A vacation in five months
Your retirement home in thirty years
Private school in four years
College in fifteen years
A down payment on a house in two years
Your winter wardrobe in three weeks

"Here are our answers, Darius," Cindy said, handing Darius a piece of paper with the following on it:

A vacation in five months:	CASH
Your retirement home in thirty years:	STOCKS
Private school in four years:	BONDS
College in fifteen years:	STOCKS
A down payment on a house in two years:	BONDS
Your winter wardrobe in three weeks:	CASH

"I would agree with you on all six, but keep in mind, there are hundreds of opinions on this subject," said Darius. "The key to asset allocation is examining your goals and seeing the big picture. For example, in your 401(k) account and your IRA account, if you decide to open one, you really should have 100 percent of your portfolio in stocks because your time horizon is more than thirty years. So, knowing what you know now, what do you plan to do Monday when you visit your company's benefits department?"

"Since I want the money to grow and I don't plan on touching it for another thirty years," said Cindy, "I plan to go to my benefits department and make sure all my assets are allocated to stocks. I don't even know what I'm investing in now, but it's going to be 100 percent in stocks starting Monday. I'm also going to make sure that the money is invested in an S&P 500 index fund, so I don't win or lose—I just match the return of the stock market!"

"Very good. You learn fast, Cindy," said Darius. "How about allocating your assets that are not in tax-deferred accounts? How do you plan on investing those?"

"I don't know, maybe a third in each?" said Scott.

"That was a trick question," said Darius. "If you take away your 401(k) money, you don't have any assets to allocate. It's not until you have eliminated all your debt and accumulated three months' worth of living expenses that you even need to worry about answering this question. Remember my Hierarchy of Investing."

After learning about the risks and rewards of investing, many of my students are tempted to start buying stocks. Some folks are so hungry to invest in the stock market that they do so before they have paid off their high-interest debt. Over the years, I have found a compromise that works well for my students. I said, "I would recommend that you start by investing $50 a month into an IRA and add this amount to your Vital Signs under the heading 'Before We Get Out of Bed.' It shows a commitment to 'paying yourself first.'"

Cindy and Scott liked the idea, but before we finished asset allocation, Cindy raised a concern: "Knowing that stocks can fluctuate, I don't know how good I would feel about putting the kids' college money in stocks."

"You've hit on a great point," said Darius. "Don't forget, as the time horizon shortens, you should choose a more conservative investment. Financial planners often talk about shifting assets from stocks to bonds as kids move closer to college age, and it's for good reason. You don't want to subject your daughter's college fund to market fluctuations right before she goes to college. In fact, six months before she goes to college, her college money should really be in cash. The same concept applies as you get closer to retirement."

Darius was right about "shifting" assets during different stages of life. It's the reason financial planners advise looking at asset allocation at least once a year. It's critical that asset choices reflect goals—especially as goals change. We were finally ready to discuss the last rule, which states: Track the performance of your investments.

Darius took it: "If you are investing in stocks, but for whatever reason you choose not to buy an index fund, be sure to compare that investment with the performance of the S&P 500. And be sure to factor taxes and commissions into your comparison. For all the bragging you hear at cocktail parties about people 'crushing' the stock market, there are very few people who actually track their investments."

I was glad Darius brought this up, and I expanded: "Part of maintaining financial wellness for a lifetime is updating your balance sheet twice a year. By looking at your assets every six months, you can track their appreciation. If the $25,000 in your 401(k) is worth $27,500 in six months, you know that your investment appreciated by 10 percent."

There are other ways to track returns. Most companies mail out a quarterly statement of 401(k) performance, and some brokerage firms do it monthly. And for those who like computers, there are a million Web sites, including my own, www.doctordink.com, that allow you to track your own portfolio and see how it is performing daily. At a minimum, I ask my students to update their balance sheet twice a year.

When Scott asked, "So how do we get started?" I knew we were ready for the last section of our outline.

Choosing an Investment Firm

I began this one, hoping to reinforce the Buyer's Antibiotic. "Remember the rule of big purchases: Always get three bids. I will give you a list of criteria for choosing an investment firm, and then you can do your own homework."

There are really three tiers of investment firms, and I knew Darius wasn't going to get bogged down in the differences. The first is deep discounters that charge less than $10 per trade. In addition to going online, some of these firms allow you to make these trades over the phone, but usually without any help from a broker. They are great for heavy traders, which most of my students are not, but they are often not very user-friendly.

Then there are the limited-service firms such as Fidelity, Charles Schwab, Vanguard, T. Rowe Price, and E-Trade. For novice investors, these firms do a great job providing some service and guidance without charging exorbitant fees. They also offer index funds with very low fees. What I like most about Fidelity and Schwab is that they have offices in most cities and can provide face-to-face service. They offer hundreds of no-load mutual funds—most with no transaction fee or up-front costs. For trading, they typically charge between $15 and $49 per trade, depending on how much you trade and how much service you require.

The last are the full-service firms, like Merrill Lynch and Solomon Smith Barney, that provide full service and very high fees. Unlike most financial advisors, I do not tell my students never to deal with a full-service broker. I just remind them that they are paying for advice and guidance and they better be getting it. If they are calling a broker simply to place a trade, they are throwing away money.

Before Darius passed out his list, I reminded Cindy and Scott of Katie's teachings: "Remember to enjoy the money you earn and stop giving it to the banks. Just as you don't want to pay unnecessary bank fees, you don't want your investment firm getting rich at your expense."

Darius nodded in agreement and we all looked over his list.

Darius's Criteria for Choosing an Investment Firm

1. A large selection of no-load mutual funds—especially index funds.
2. Low fees for buying mutual funds and stocks.
3. Low minimum-investment requirements.
4. Automatic withdrawal from personal accounts to purchase investments.
5. Customer service—by phone, Internet, or in person, depending on your comfort level.
6. If you are dealing with a full-service broker, make sure you have good chemistry and a high level of trust.

The list was fairly self-explanatory, but Darius added, "The automatic withdrawal from your personal accounts is a critical criteria. The best way to pay yourself first is to have money taken directly out of your checking account, or your paycheck, and put into an investment. I got my little brother to start putting $75 per month into an IRA, and he has already seen his investment grow. Even better, he tells me that he doesn't even notice that the money is gone."

As usual, Darius had hit on a great point, and we were just about ready to wrap up. The only item left was the importance of the Internet. I recalled an incident when Michelle and I were both online and she was shopping for a textbook. She e-mailed me to ask if I knew of any discount bookstores, and after doing a Google search, I found a site called cheapbooks.com. After she bought the book, Michelle sent me this e-mail: "Dr. Dink is going to love this. I got three bids for the books—$90.23, $92.60, and the last one, $65.20 from cheapbooks.com."

I shared this story with the group, and Darius commented, "Information sharing is deflationary."

"What the heck is that supposed to mean, Mr. Alan Greenspan?" mocked Cindy, referring to the head of the Federal Reserve, who talks about inflation as often as Imelda Marcos buys a new pair of shoes.

"It means that when you share information, the price of items goes down," said Darius. "Using the Internet and taking advantage of technology is a great way to save money and make money. Whether you are using a price-comparison site like mysimon.com or going to fool.com to learn how to negotiate the purchase of a car, there are so many great financial tools at your disposal. And to keep up with your financial therapy, don't forget about doctordink.com," said Darius, in reference to my very own Web site, which students have found to be a great tool for maintaining financial health.

As Michelle had learned, Darius was right. I'm not one for fancy computer programs, but the Internet has proven to be an incredible tool. Because I use e-mail so much, my phone bills have gone down and I'm even more in touch with my friends, family, and students. And on the investment side, I save time and money by making my investments and doing my research online.

As we prepared to leave, Darius asked Scott to read a small piece of an article written by Jonathan Clements for *The Wall Street Journal* on July 27, 1999. We had both agreed that it would be a great way to conclude, and Scott obliged.

> An investment portfolio's growth is driven by how much we save, how long we invest, what return we earn, and how much of that return we surrender to investment costs and to taxes. Think of this as your formula for investment success.
>
> We have an enormous amount of control over every factor in the formula, except one. So guess which factor consumes most of your energies?
>
> Yup, you've got it.
>
> Investors spend an absurd amount of time trying to control the one thing they can do the least about, which is their raw investment performance. They attempt to pick hot stocks, find star fund managers, and guess the market's direction. Yet it is extraordinarily difficult, if not impossible, to do any of these things. . . .
>
> Just because it is critical, however, doesn't mean we can do much about it. The reality is, we can help our portfolio's growth far more by increasing savings, investing longer, and cutting investment costs and taxes.

Darius loved that article because it so easily summarized the essentials of investing. He knew how hard it was to beat the market, yet he saw how much time, effort, and money people spent trying to beat it. Before Cindy and Scott left, he wanted to reinforce what he had taught them. "The article sums up my own philosophy on investing—*invest in yourself, increase your savings, take advantage of the power of compound interest, and try to match the market by using index funds.*"

Cindy and Scott nodded their heads in agreement and thanked Darius. We left Darius's office, took the subway to the Port Authority, then hopped a bus to La Guardia for our flight home. The heavy air in New York City never seemed clearer as Cindy and Scott left the Big Apple with a firm understanding of the risks and rewards of investing. The only thing that would have made the trip better was if we'd had time to stop at Carnegie Deli and grab a giant corned beef sandwich.

Exercise 8
Revise Your Vital Signs

Now that you've gone through the first seven steps of financial therapy, it's time to revise your vital signs.

Monthly Vital Signs	Before Therapy	After Therapy
What's Coming In		
Take-home pay from primary jobs		
Other income		
TOTAL INFLOWS		
What's Going Out—Before We Get Out of Bed		
Paying ourselves first—IRA contribution		
Rent/mortgage		
Basic utilities—electricity, gas, water, basic phone		
Renter's/homeowner's insurance		
Car insurance—car 1		
Car insurance—car 2		
Life insurance (do not add if already taken out of take-home pay)		
Additional medical insurance, including dental		
Car payment 1		
Car payment 2		
Other monthly payments		
Credit card payments		
Student loans		
TOTAL WHAT'S GOING OUT—BEFORE WE GET OUT OF BED		
What's Going Out—Basic Necessities		
Groceries—in-home eating		
Basic clothing		
Gas and car maintenance		
Child care		
Other—dry cleaning, laundry, cleaning supplies, etc.		
Pet-related expenses		
TOTAL WHAT'S GOING OUT—BASIC NECESSITIES		
What's Going Out—If You Had to Live Without		
Long-distance phone		
Cable, basic and additional movie channels		
Clothes and other shopping goodies		
Toys, videos, music		
Eating out		
Cell phones		
Household services—cleaning, lawn care		
TOTAL IF YOU HAD TO LIVE WITHOUT		
TOTAL INFLOWS		
TOTAL OUTFLOWS		
MONTHLY SURPLUS (DEFICIT)		

Chapter 9

Maintain Financial Wellness for a Lifetime

There isn't a part of our lives that money doesn't touch—it affects our relationships, the way we go about our everyday activities, our ability to make dreams reality, everything. Most of us, I think, have a core anxiety that we carry around with us, though we may not admit it to ourselves. That is part of money's power over us.

—Suze Orman

As a young kid, my Grandpa Harry was always trying to make a better life for his mom. He started selling newspapers when he was only nine, and he was constantly picking up odd jobs around the neighborhood. When the other people on the block started to get indoor plumbing, he wanted his mom to have it too. In fact, he wanted it so much that he was prepared to fight, literally. So one day he came home with a huge black eye and a swollen nose, and his mom was terrified. The first thing out of her mouth was "You bum, you no-good street-fightin' fool—you'll never make anything out of yourself."

What she didn't know was that her fifteen-year-old son was an aspiring boxer and, with the nickname "Kid Canvas," had started boxing for money. When his mom finally stopped yelling at him, he had time to say, "But Mom, I made fifteen dollars."

Without skipping a beat, she said, "So when's your next fight?"

I've asked my ninety-one-year-old grandfather to tell me that story over and over, and it just gets better and better. After I returned from New York, I was thinking a lot about my grandpa Harry since he's always been such a great model for maintaining financial wellness for a lifetime. The lessons he has shared with me over the years have been priceless. He made more than he spent each month, invested in index funds, and always managed to find a way to buy things wholesale. Moreover, he always reminded me that if a deal seems too good to be true, it usually is. Over the years, he had seen his fair share of scams and learned that get-rich schemes only make the person running the scheme rich. His good decisions have allowed him to maintain excellent health, both physically and financially.

My purpose for this last session was to make sure my students saw this as the beginning, and not the end, of financial wellness. Without enough frequent-flyer miles to fly to Baltimore and spend an afternoon with Grandpa Harry, I decided we should meet one last time at Java Road. Michelle had promised to stop by and help teach this session, but when she would actually show up was anyone's guess.

Before Michelle arrived, Cindy and Scott joined me at my regular booth and we started by taking a look at their revised Vital Signs. Cindy was practically blushing when she passed them to me, so I knew there was good news.

Monthly Vital Signs	Before Therapy	After Therapy
What's Coming In		
Take-home pay from primary jobs	3,000	3,000
Cindy's raise, 50 cents/hour	0	60
Scott's two weekend shifts	0	216
Other income, Friday-night baby-sitting	0	210
Pet-sitting business	0	100
TOTAL INFLOWS	**$3,000**	**$3,586**

What's Going Out—Before We Get Out of Bed	**Before Therapy**	**After Therapy**
Paying ourselves first—IRA contribution	0	50
Rent/mortgage	900	900
Basic utilities—electricity, gas, water, basic phone	135	135
Renter's/homeowner's insurance	15	15
Car insurance—car 1	100	80
Car insurance—car 2	80	60
Life insurance (do not add if already taken out of take-home pay)	25	0
Additional medical insurance, including dental	25	0
Car payments—minivan	325	325
Car payments—convertible	275	275
Credit card payments	290	207
Student loans	150	150
TOTAL WHAT'S GOING OUT—BEFORE WE GET OUT OF BED	**$2,320**	**2,197**
What's Going Out—Basic Necessities		
Groceries—in-home eating	520	440
Basic clothing	150	70
Gas and car maintenance	200	200
Child care	280	140
Other—dry cleaning, laundry, cleaning supplies, etc.	50	30
Pet-related expenses	50	50
TOTAL WHAT'S GOING OUT—BASIC NECESSITIES	**$1,250**	**930**
What's Going Out—If You Had to Live Without		
Long-distance phone	120	50
Cable, basic and additional movie channels	50	20
Clothes and other shopping goodies	180	80
Toys, videos, music	80	40
Eating out	100	75
Cell phones	120	60
Household services—cleaning, lawn care	0	0
Charity	NAF	20
Gifts—weddings, birthdays, anniversaries	NAF	60
Travel	NAF	50
TOTAL IF YOU HAD TO LIVE WITHOUT	**$650**	**455**
TOTAL INFLOWS	**$3,000**	**$3,586**
TOTAL OUTFLOWS	**$4,220**	**$3,582**
MONTHLY SURPLUS (DEFICIT)	**$(1,220)**	**$4**

Seeing a surplus at the bottom of the page got me excited, but I was a little thrown off when I saw "NAF" in the old column. Cindy explained, "It stands for Not Accounted For. Scott and I realized that we always have all these one-time expenses, and we wanted a way to budget for these things each month."

"I'm sorry for not bringing it up earlier," I said. "One of the biggest mistakes many of my students make is not accounting for *everything* in their Vital Signs. Then, when they overspend, they often attribute it to special occasions. When you don't account for all of your outflows, it seems like every month there will be a *special* occasion."

"Like December, for example," said Scott. "We know we are going to spend more than $60 for Christmas presents, but when we 'added it up to the reality,' we decided that $720 should be enough for presents for the entire year. And while we're not thrilled with having a total of only $600 a year for travel, we know that's all we can afford."

I was really impressed with their observations, and even happier to see that they had included charity. Just like paying yourself first, including charity in your Vital Signs is a great start, even if it's only a small amount. Cindy commented, "I'd actually like to give a little more to charity and less to the credit companies, and in due time, I think that will be possible."

"You are certainly on your way," I said. "Another suggestion is to give to charity by giving your time rather than your money. Many religions support the notion that you should give 10 percent of your income to charity. But if that's not possible, a fair trade-off is to give 10 percent of your work hours to charity—an additional four hours per week."

Cindy liked the idea, and it was now time to talk about making this work. "Rather than me tell you how to maintain financial health, I have invited a special guest," I said as Michelle walked over to our booth.

"I might have come late, but I don't come cheap," said Michelle as she sat down at our booth.

Everyone took a moment to get caught up, and I slipped away to get Michelle her prearranged payment, a croissant with butter and strawberry jam and a cup of Earl Grey tea. More than anyone I know, Michelle understands that maintaining sound financial health requires a lifelong commitment. Just as she had to juggle the cost of raising two young kids with getting her degree, she now has to juggle the cost of living in the expensive city of Boston, child care, and presenting a professional image at her job. It's a struggle, but Michelle always seems to find a way, and I knew she could transfer this knowledge to Cindy and Scott.

Michelle got right down to business. "I always try to write checks or use cash to pay for things. I don't even have a credit card anymore—it's just too tempting. I have found that by writing checks I'm able to keep track of my spending, and I don't have to worry about spending money that I don't have. Plus, after seeing how much I wasted over the years in bank fees, I wouldn't dare bounce a check or go below my monthly minimum. And when I have to pay cash, it pains me so much to part with it that I'm much more responsible about spending. When I had credit cards, I didn't even think twice."

"What about putting cash equal to my budget in an envelope for all of our various expenses?" asked Scott. "That way, we know to stop spending when we run out."

"Not a bad idea, and if it helps you stay within your budget, go for it," said Michelle. "Dr. Dink always stresses that you have to do what works for you."

Michelle was right that I do in fact tell my students to do what works for them. Some of my students like to set up a bunch of different accounts to keep savings separate for a house or even a new computer or a vacation. For those who don't carry credit card balances, like my parents, it makes sense to use a credit card, because they can earn bonus points and keep a record of all their expenses.

Michelle continued: "And always make sure to pay yourself first. I have it set up with my bank that at the beginning of every month, the bank takes $50 out of my account for my IRA and another $50 for each of my kids' college funds. I also have a direct payment of $80 for my student loans so that I don't miss a payment and mess up my credit rating. That way I don't have to worry about having money left over at the end of the month for saving—I take it all out up front. I'm the kind of person that if I had the money in my account, I would spend it."

"Not the Godiva chocolate queen," I joked, to which Michelle shot me a smirk. If there is one thing I know about Michelle, it's that money has a tendency to burn a hole in her pocket. I find that most of my students are the same way. It's the reason that when people ask me for a strategy for gambling in Las Vegas, I tell them to have access to as little cash as possible. Even Steve Wynn, the man who built the Mirage and the Bellagio, said, "If you want to make money in a casino—own one!" Bringing a small amount of cash and leaving the ATM card at home is the best form of preventive medicine I know.

"What about rewarding ourselves, Michelle?" asked Cindy. "Don't you think that an incentive would make it easier to achieve our goals?"

"Absolutely. There's no question you should reward yourself, but the beauty of creating realistic Vital Signs is that the rewards are already included," said Michelle.

"Maybe I'm blind, but I don't see a column called 'Rewards' under Outflows," said Cindy.

"First of all, feel free to add one—they are *your* Vital Signs," said Michelle, sounding a lot like me. "The idea of the Vital Signs is not to make your life miserable to the point where you want to splurge. By incorporating travel and gifts, you already have rewarded yourself in a way. If you don't think your Vital Signs are realistic, then you might as well start from scratch."

"We just can't believe," said Scott, "that we erased a deficit of $1,220 and have money to pay ourselves first, travel, and buy gifts. We're kind of in denial—kind of like the credit card debt denial that we were in before you introduced us to Dr. Dink."

"I'm sure you had to give up a few things in order to have positive Vital Signs," said Michelle, "but more than anything, you made good choices that will allow you to accomplish your goals. There's no sense beating yourself up for having been in such bad shape. But now that you have been through financial therapy, there are no more excuses."

"I think we can handle checking the Vital Signs once a month," said Cindy. "What else do we need to do to maintain good financial health?"

"The other thing you need to do, twice a year, is re-create your financial vision and revise your balance sheet," said Michelle. "I don't get any satisfaction when I write those checks to pay off my debt, but I feel great when I see after six months that the 'Assets' column keeps going up and the 'Liabilities' column keeps going down."

At this point, Michelle had provided all the information that Cindy and Scott needed to maintain financial wellness for a lifetime. Writing down Vital Signs monthly, and taking the time every six months to revise the balance sheet and re-create the vision, is all that it really takes. When I say that maintaining financial wellness for a lifetime requires only a half-hour commitment once a month and an extra half hour every six months, I mean it.

The Ritual

One of the interesting things about Michelle is the ritual that she performs every month when it comes time to write down her Vital Signs. "On the last Saturday of every month," she explained, "I put the kids in the car and drive around my favorite neighborhoods—looking at for-sale signs on houses. This reminds me of my dream of owning a home and that I must make good decisions in order to achieve that dream. Then I go to the mall and get Häagen-Dazs ice cream—always vanilla for me and Rocky Road for my son, Logan; Thea is still too young for her own scoop, so she just picks from both of ours. The ice cream allows me to enjoy the moment and reminds me that there are many of life's simple pleasures that I can enjoy without spending a lot of money."

As I was thinking about how effective her ritual is, Michelle continued: "After I go 'house shopping' and eat my Häagen-Dazs, I take the kids to the park and break out my Vital Signs. As I watch them run around—oh my God, they are so cute together—I look at my Vital Signs from the previous month and see how things went. I can look at the balance in my checking account and compare it to the previous month's. Because all of my expenses and investments come right out of my checking account, I know that as long as the balance stays the same, I have met my goal. Then I go to work on the next month. Being at a park and seeing my kids run around puts me at peace and reminds me of why I am working so hard."

To check her results from the previous month, Michelle uses an easy technique. She keeps $700 in her checking account and knows that she cannot fall below her minimum balance of $500 without incurring any fees. Because all her inflows—including her paycheck, which is directly deposited into her checking account—and all her outflows—including her monthly investments—go in and out of this one account, she can look at the ending balances from month to month to see how she did. If her balance is $660 one month, she knows that she went over by $40 and tries to make up for that the following month. If her account says $775, she'll take a few bucks and treat herself to something and use the rest to contribute to the kids' college fund.

Michelle's ritual is consistent with one of the most effective ways to achieve goals: making them visual. For Michelle, it's the for-sale signs that keep her on track each month and the pictures of her kids on her desk at work. For my friend Zubs, it's keeping a picture of a boat in his wallet. My buddy Charles, who is an architect, went so far as to create blueprints for his dream home, which he framed and hung on his bedroom wall. My friend Robin keeps an old credit card statement with a zero balance on her fridge to remind her of how good she felt when she didn't have any debt.

Prescription Review

Over the course of financial therapy, so much material had been presented to Cindy and Scott that I wanted to be sure they retained it all. Michelle and I had spent about an hour on the phone going over what we should review. We decided to pick a few things from each step and ask a few questions to make sure the important stuff was still on the tips of their tongues.

I started with the questioning: "Why do you think I had you come listen to me speak for your first session of therapy?"

"Because you wanted to show us that making good decisions is the key to financial wellness," said Cindy. "Your examples about car shopping, education, and buying a home really brought home the importance of Q-Q-Kachoo. We learned on the first day that we must always do the numbers, consult Ben Franklin, and check our gut before we make a big decision."

This was going to be easy, I thought to myself after hearing Cindy's perfect description. Without even being asked, Scott said, "Once you taught us Q-Q-Kachoo, you made us create our vision of financial wellness. Seeing our goals and dreams on paper, and seeing that the way we were living was far from what financial wellness looks like to us, inspired us to go through each step. You were right that there are no shortcuts."

A part of me wanted to stop right there. If there's anything my students need to remember, it is that *taking the time to write down what you really want in life and making good decisions are the keys to financial wellness.*

Nonetheless, we still had work to do and Michelle was ready to review the session on big purchases. I thought about how lucky we were to have my brother, a career salesman, teach all the insider's tricks. Michelle said, "The next thing you need to do is watch your major purchases. It is very easy to get lazy and not shop around. Don't forget what Dr. Dink taught you: *The bigger the purchase, the more time you should spend.* And by the way, can you explain the Buyer's Antibiotic?"

"It's a form Dr. Dink and his brother created to avoid all the nonsense of dealing with salespeople," said Scott. "We know we have to get three bids, and this form helps us make sure we can compare apples to apples and know exactly what we are buying."

After this perfect answer, my thoughts turned to Katie, and I asked Cindy a question that she no doubt had the answer to. "What's Katie's motto?"

" 'Enjoy the Money You Earn—Stop Giving It to the Banks'," said Cindy. "Katie taught us that we shouldn't have any loans with an interest rate above 10 percent. She also reminded us that wasting money on things like late fees and parking tickets takes away from things we can enjoy for ourselves."

Right on, I thought. As for Erl's session on making more than you spend every month—the Vital Signs—I had already written out her best list on a prescription card, and I had Michelle read it aloud.

The Finance Doctor

℞

Erl's Seven "Hows" of Financial Health

1. How much you make.
2. How much you spend.
3. How much goes out for interest, fees, and taxes.
4. How you make decisions for major purchases.
5. How much you invest.
6. How long you invest the money.
7. How you invest the money.

Dr. Dink, MBA

After turning a $1,220 deficit into a surplus, I did not think Erl's lessons would soon be forgotten. When Vital Signs show a deficit, it's critical to find ways to improve inflows and outflows in order to close the gap. Erl gave them a bunch of commonsense suggestions that, when added up, really made a difference.

Interrupting my thoughts, Michelle said, "How lucky that you got to go to New York for a field trip. What did you learn in the Big Apple?"

"Before we even left," said Cindy, "we learned that a balance sheet is like our financial résumé. We also learned that while our net worth is positive, just about all of our assets are illiquid, and most of our liabilities carry too high of an interest rate. Once we arrived, Dr. Lori showed us how the Rule of 72 can turn us into millionaires by taking advantage of compound interest. By investing our 401(k) money wisely and using dollar cost averaging to contribute to an IRA, we will almost certainly retire with over a million dollars in savings."

Wow, Dr. Lori did a great job, I thought. "And what did you learn from that Wall Street hotshot?" asked Michelle, who knew I always counted on Darius, either by phone or in person, to help my students understand the risks and rewards of investing.

"We first learned what the stock market is, and then learned that there are no free lunches in investing," said Scott. "He showed us the difference between stocks, bonds, and cash, and the risks and rewards of each investment. After explaining how mutual funds work, he showed us why we should invest in an index of the S&P 500 as a way to grow our assets."

Cindy added, "He also taught us some Wall Street terminology like 'Dow Jones,' 'NASDAQ 100,' and 'bullish versus bearish.' Even more important, he emphasized that the best investment we can make is in ourselves. Before we left, he gave us the necessary tips on choosing an investment firm and how to utilize the Internet to save money."

At that point, we had gone through all 8 steps and I felt confident that Cindy and Scott really understood financial therapy. Utilizing guest speakers and taking field trips turned out to be just the prescription that Cindy and Scott needed. A list person herself, Michelle wanted to leave one final reminder that included all her suggestions for maintaining financial wellness for a lifetime.

Michelle's Reminders for Maintaining Financial Wellness for a Lifetime

1. Go through all three steps of Q-Q-Kachoo for important decisions.
2. Create your vision, make your goals visual, and share it with the right "dreaming crabs."
3. Spend a "fun" half an hour every month on your Vital Signs.
4. Revise your balance sheet every six months and fight to get rid of high-interest debt.
5. Don't get lazy—use your Buyer's Antibiotic for major purchases.
6. Pay yourself first by dollar cost averaging into a tax-deferred account.

As we started packing our things up to take off, Cindy said to Michelle, "I have one more question for you. What should we invest in once our cars are paid off and we have extra money in our Vital Signs?"

"The great thing about financial therapy is that you can answer that question yourself," said Michelle. "It all comes back to your goals. As much as I want to travel, wear nicer clothes, and eat more chocolate, my number-one priority is my kids' education. So if I have extra cash, it goes right to the college fund. Goals do change, so re-creating your vision every six months is just as essential as revising your balance sheet."

"You are just like Dr. Dink," said Cindy. "We ask you where you think we should invest our money and you tell us that it all comes back to our goals. Why can't you just once give us a simple answer?"

"Because if she did," I chimed in while Michelle was busy inhaling her croissant, "I'd think you hadn't truly mastered financial therapy. Because I can never account for every scenario that life will present you, I did my best to provide you with a foundation to *make your own decisions.* If you asked me whether it made more sense to invest $300 in the stock market or to pay off your high-interest debt, what do you think I would say?"

"You would tell us that one of the rules of investing is that we can't have any high-interest debt and we must have three months of living expenses before we even think about putting money in the stock market," said Cindy. "Then you would tell us that we shouldn't invest in stocks if we are going to need the money in the next couple of years. Then, before coming up for air, you would tell us to examine our goals and think about how important owning a home and education are to us."

"That's impressive, Cindy. Would you ever consider working for me?" I asked with a smile.

"Not until I find out my market value first," she said. "You might not be able to afford me!"

With that answer, I knew Michelle and I had accomplished our goal. We had not only reviewed all 8 Steps, but also explained how to maintain financial wellness for a lifetime. Just as Michelle had developed her own ritual, I was sure Cindy and Scott would as well. As for me, I was finally ready to take a vacation.

Before we said good-bye, I gave Cindy and Scott their final set of exercises.

Exercise 9

Spend a half hour each month on your Vital Signs—review the previous month and fill out the following month.

Every six months:
Re-create your vision for financial wellness.
Revise your balance sheet.

Epilogue

Perfect freedom is reserved for the man who lives by his own work and in that work does what he wants to do.

—R. G. Collingwood

I never was able to break away for that vacation. Cindy and Scott kept sending me their friends, and I was one busy doctor. On a rare day off, about six months after my last session with Cindy and Scott, I was sitting at Java Road, trying to relax with a John Irving novel, when I noticed a familiar face staring at me. I put my glasses on and realized that it was Cindy's brother, Brent—whom I hadn't seen since our field trip with Katie.

Apparently Brent recognized me, because he and his wife practically sprinted over to my booth, just as Brent had sprinted out of the mall that day to go day-trade. "This is my wife, Caitlin," Brent said, "and she and I decided that we are ready for financial therapy. I got that home equity loan, but with all the money I lost day trading, we are in danger of losing our house. We even had one of our cars repossessed."

I felt bad hearing this, especially since I had a hunch it was coming. Although emergency care is not part of my practice, I knew I had to offer some assistance before it was too late. Just as I was pondering a prescription, Cindy and Scott showed up and announced, "Today is our six-month anniversary of completing financial therapy! We figured we'd re-create our vision and revise our balance sheet at good old Java Road. How ironic it is that we ran into Brent, Caitlin, and Dr. Dink."

I didn't think it was ironic. In fact, I couldn't think of anything more fitting on a day off than running into two former students and a couple in need of emergency care. "How's your market value?" I said to Cindy, playing a hunch.

"I explored the job market," she said, "and I did find out that I could make more money somewhere else, but after negotiating flex-time with my boss, I decided to stay. It's wound up saving me money on child care, and it's much less stressful."

The last time we met, we joked about the idea of Cindy working for me, but what she didn't realize is that I wasn't joking. Over the years, I've found that the best teachers are usually the most difficult students. Because Cindy was in such financial chaos when I met her, and still had succeeded as a student, I knew she had the makings of a great teacher. And with a brother in danger of losing everything, I had found her first student—even though she didn't know it yet.

I decided to ease her into her role, hoping Scott would take the bait as well, and said, "Can you guys tell Brent and Caitlin the six reminders that Michelle gave you for maintaining financial wellness for a lifetime?"

"Not only can we tell you, we can show you," said Scott, pulling a laminated piece of paper out of his wallet. "You talked about making goals visual, so one of the things I do is keep Michelle's list in my wallet at all times. That way, every time I go to spend money, I'm reminded of what I need to do."

Scott passed the piece of paper to Caitlin, and I asked her to read it aloud.

Michelle's Reminders for Maintaining Financial Wellness for a Lifetime

1. Go through all three steps of Q-Q-Kachoo for important decisions.
2. Create your vision, make your goals visual, and share it with the right "dreaming crabs."
3. Spend a "fun" half an hour every month on your Vital Signs.
4. Revise your balance sheet every six months and fight to get rid of high-interest debt.
5. Don't get lazy—use your Buyer's Antibiotic for major purchases.
6. Pay yourself first by dollar cost averaging into a tax-deferred account.

Just as I had anticipated, this list set off a million questions. Brent wanted to know what Q-Q-Kachoo meant, and Caitlin kept asking about the Vital Signs. Rather than interrupt, I let Cindy and Scott field these questions while I tried to get back to my book. Within minutes, I was going through my files, looking for a form that said "Diagnosis" on the top. After I fished it out and handed it to Cindy, I heard her and Scott firing away with questions: "If we had more money, we would spend it on . . . ? If we didn't have to work, we would spend our time . . . ? Where does it hurt now?"

Just like that, I had turned two of my prized students into two potentially great teachers. While those four continued to talk, I decided to look through my files on creating a vision and found the first one I had ever created for myself. Seeing Cindy and Scott so eager to share their knowledge put me on top of the world. When I looked at my vision, I realized that none of this was an accident.

All of a sudden, I felt the need to share. While I often tell stories about my family and share personal anecdotes, I try to stay focused on the students. But when I looked at this piece of paper, I wanted to show the group the power of creating a vision and how it made an impact on my life.

When Cindy finally came up for air, I said, "I want to share the vision that I created for myself on October 27, 1993, just after I graduated from college." I read:

> I look forward to waking up every day and embarking on a project that brings out my competitive nature and desire to help others. I get up when I want, work when I want, and make my own decisions. What I'm doing is important and has a purpose. I am constantly in win-win situations, because what I do makes others happy. I set goals and achieve goals because I work smarter, not harder. I am able to enjoy my work, because it is in harmony with my values and doesn't negatively affect the other aspects of my life. I keep my competitive spirit alive by setting the goalposts for success myself and not worrying about the Joneses. I love life.

After reading, I looked down on this piece of paper and saw that I had also written down "Completed by 29th birthday." I didn't think it was any coincidence that my twenty-ninth birthday was less than a month away. Through all the financial and professional ups and downs, I had always referred back to this vision, and it shaped everything I did.

Between helping Michelle graduate and finding her dream job as an interior designer, getting out of "the trap" by eliminating $25,000 worth of credit card debt, and teaching Cindy and Scott financial wellness *and* how to share that knowledge with others, I knew I was living my professional dream.

With Caitlin and Brent in good hands, I decided to pack up my things and head to the park. Before I left, I couldn't help but offer one last bit of advice: "Don't get ahead of yourselves," I said. "Remember that prescription without diagnosis is malpractice!"

Afterword

When all is said and done, there is more said than done.
—Lou Holtz

I hope after reading this book that this quote does not hold true for you. If you skipped over the exercises, please go back and perform them. A half an hour a month and an extra half an hour every six months is all it takes. Don't let Dr. Dink down!

Dr. Dink's Glossary of Concepts and Terms

ADD IT UP TO THE REALITY—Don't let a salesperson suck you in by breaking the overall price down into small payments. Always figure out the total purchase price before you buy anything. If they say thirty bucks a month, you think $360 a year.

BEDSIDE MANNER—Just about every student I meet has a fear of looking dumb, and they all seem to think that they are the only ones who are ignorant on the topic of finance. It is my job to exhibit good "bedside manner" and answer all their questions patiently.

BUYER'S ANTIBIOTIC—Since you have better things to do than listen to a bunch of hullabaloo, my brother and I created a simple form for you to use when you are getting three bids on major purchases.

DOLLAR COST AVERAGING—This is an effective way of investing, in which you invest a set dollar amount every month. It provides protection against the market's ups and downs.

DR. DINK UTOPIA (D-D-U)—D-D-U is getting to a place in life where all decisions are made as if money is not an issue.

DREAMING CRABS—The story of the "Three Dreaming Crabs" reminds you to think about who embraces your dreams and to share your vision with those people. And just as important, be sure to stay away from the cancerous crabs in your life who only want to pull you down and prevent you from chasing your dreams.

ENJOY THE MONEY YOU EARN—Katie's motto reminds you that when you waste money out of sheer laziness, by forgetting to make a payment on time, or by getting a bank fee for a bounced check, you are simply taking away the chance to buy something that will make you feel good.

FINANCIAL THERAPY—An 8-step prescription that adds a little structure to the common sense that you already have.

GOOD FINANCIAL HEALTH—Good financial health means being in the position to chase your dreams instead of your bills.

INDEX FUND—An index fund is a mutual fund that mirrors the performance of a market index, such as the S&P 500, the Dow Jones, or the NASDAQ 100. The advantage is that you will earn the same return as the index while paying very low fees.

PAY YOURSELF FIRST—It's painless, yet it's something that so few of us do. Each month, you should pay yourself first by having a set amount automatically withdrawn from your paycheck or checking account and put directly into an investment, such as an index fund.

Q-Q-KACHOO—The three-step formula for decision making that my mom created. The first Q stands for Quantitative—doing the numbers. The second Q stands for Qualitative—doing a Ben Franklin by listing the pros and cons. And the Kachoo reminds you to check your gut.

RULE OF 72—Dr. Lori explained this rule to emphasize the power of compounding. To apply this rule, divide 72 by your rate of return to see how long it will take to double your money. If you earn 12 percent, your money will double every six years.

SELLING OUT—People "sell out" when they get so overwhelmed by their bills that they give up on their dreams to make ends meet. It becomes a vicious cycle where a person compromises his or her passions in life because he or she is so worried about paying the bills.

SUCCESSFUL STUDENT—A successful student is one who meets the goals that they have outlined.

THE TRAP—See SELLING OUT.

TAX-DEFERRED ACCOUNTS—Accounts such as your 401(k) or IRA allow your money to grow tax-free. By taking advantage of tax-deferred accounts, you save a fortune in taxes and grow your assets considerably faster.

VISION OF FINANCIAL WELLNESS—Creating a vision starts by identifying what financial wellness looks like. The second step is to write down goals that meet these four criteria. Goals must be *specific*, *challenging*, *attainable*, and *have a deadline*. Then list your dreams. Dreams remind you of why you are working so hard and that anything is possible.

VITAL SIGNS—The most important element in your financial health is making more than you spend every month. That's why I refer to your monthly budget as your Vital Signs.

Resources

Reading *The Finance Doctor* should be seen as the start to a lifetime of knowledge and smart decision making. The following are some resources to help you along your continued journey.

Dr. Dink's Favorite Web Sites for Learning and Saving Money

1. www.doctordink.com	Outlines financial therapy and includes forms for all the exercises
2. www.mysimon.com	Allows you to compare prices on just about everything
3. www.priceline.com	You can pick your price—works great for travel
4. www.fool.com	The mission of the Motley Fool is to educate, amuse, and enrich
5. www.edmunds.com	Loaded with information about cars
6. www.taxsites.com	A great start for any questions on taxes

7.	www.ebay.com	An online auction where you can be a buyer or a seller
8.	www.consumerreports.org	An independent source of information with no ads
9.	www.fastweb.com	Helps you find more than $1 billion in college scholarship information
10.	www.nelliemae.com	Answers all your questions about student loans
11.	www.productopia.com	Experts offer unbiased advice on popular products
12.	www.investorwords.com	More than 5,000 definitions and 15,000 links between related terms

A Dozen Books for Finance, Fun, and Life

1. *Free to Choose,* Milton and Rose Friedman
2. *The Armchair Economist: Economics and Everyday Life,* Steven E. Landsburg
3. *The Motley Fool Investment Guide,* David and Tom Gardner
4. *The Alchemist,* Paulo Coelho
5. *The Sales Bible,* Jeffrey H. Gitomer
6. *Vitale,* Dick Vitale with Curry Kirkpatrick
7. *One Up on Wall Street,* Peter Lynch
8. *The Monk and the Riddle,* Randy Komisar
9. *The 7 Habits of Highly Effective People,* Stephen R. Covey
10. *The Road Less Traveled,* M. Scott Peck
11. *Real Poker: The Cooke Collection,* Roy Cooke and John Bond
12. *Body for Life,* Bill Phillips

Acknowledgments

As I was writing this book, my friends and family became my proofreaders, and they helped shape it. Special thanks to Jimmy Haley, Pete Fornatale, Jennifer Thornton, Cari Ugent, Shannon McLinden, Scott McLinden, Charles Weisenberg, Jason Freeland, Steve Mitzenmacher, Brett Silver, Jackie Davis, Scott Hirsch, John Whittington, Ryan Hadlock, Brad Bernatek, Barry Blanken, Todd Burski, Alexandra Como, the Woods, Jill and Bob Batler, Jimmy and Susan Kemp, Jon and Keelan Bodow, Jeremy and Robin London, Mark and Shan Meulenberg, Monica and Rich Levine, Audrey and Spero Alex, Brad and Sherri Bosart, Bobert and Heidi Cohen, Todd and Judy Solan, and Jon and Caryn Rehme.

Teachers, coaches, and bosses have made a huge impact in my life and ultimately help shape the way I teach. I especially want to thank Coach Wilbert Givins, Mr. Baker, Señora Silvia, Marty Berger, Todd Archibald, Coach Grandi, Mrs. Rasmussen, Coach Kuhayda, Coach Foringer, Coach Shepherd, Coach Tapley, Coach Karasinski, David Brooks, Gary Lancz, Dr. William Boyes, Dr. George Gallinger, Bob Schmidt, Janet Acheatel, and Kathi Baker.

I want to thank Hubie Balsamic for introducing me to Frank Scatoni, and Stephanie Carter for introducing me to Lisa Hoffacker. I never understood the true power of networking until I met these two. Lisa's creative design was matched only by her perpetual support. Frank showed me why I wasn't as good a writer as I thought I was and urged me to tell my story.

I also want to thank Dr. Donna Blancero, for giving me the chance that launched my career; Tom Hughes, for a seemingly endless supply of great quotes and heartfelt enthusiasm; Richie Applebaum, for unconditional support and a model for success; and Michelle Charles, for being my best friend, the mother of my precious god-kids, and for whom financial therapy was created.

Personally, I want to give credit to Mike Kelly, Lori Marcus, Pete Crosby, Tim Simpson, Ivonne Polasky, Jack Gonzalez, and the Knopps, Hites, and Greenes for keeping me sane while I was living in New York City.

Above all, I want to thank my family, who have always been able to laugh at my idiosyncrasies and tolerate my frequent address changes.

Index

About the Authors

DR. DINK is a writer and a financial therapist who loves to teach. He has a B.S. from Cornell University and an M.B.A. from Arizona State University. He currently resides in Santa Monica, California, and will talk to anyone who will listen about how to stop chasing their bills and start chasing their dreams. The best way to reach him is by e-mail at askdoctordink@aol.com or through his Web site at www.doctordink.com.

FRANK R. SCATONI is the coauthor of two pop culture books, *Who Can It Be Now?* and *Say Anything.* He is a frequent contributor to several high-profile Web sites, including Rouze.com and Backslap.com, and his work has been featured in *Cosmopolitan, Entertainment Weekly,* and *Maxim* magazines. This is his first book with the esteemed Dr. Dink.